THE TWENTY-FIRST CENTURY
DEACON AND DEACONESS

This book is the author's published proceedings from his doctoral dissertation, presented in partial fulfillment of the requirements for the Doctor of Ministry degree in Leadership at Andrews University Theological Seminary, Berrien Springs, MI in December 2010.

THE TWENTY-FIRST CENTURY DEACON AND DEACONESS

REFLECTING THE BIBLICAL MODEL

Foreword by Elder J. Alfred Johnson, II

Vincent E. White, Sr.

Published by
AVA's Book Publishers
109 Ellacott Drive
Huntsville, AL 35806

Dr. Vincent E. White, Sr. is an ordained minister, and has served as a pastor in the Seventh-day Adventist church for twenty-seven years. He has conducted deacon and deaconess training seminars throughout North America, and is the author of *Problem Solvers and Soul Winners: A Handbook for Deacons and Deaconesses*, AVA's Book Publishers, 1999.

AVA's Book Publishers
109 Ellacott Drive
Huntsville, AL 35806
www.avasbookpublishers.com

Cover design by S & V Graphic Designing Service, www.svgraphicdesigning.com
Mirror image, courtesy of the Stanley Weiss Collection, www.stanleyweiss.com

Printed and bound in the United States of America

Second Impression: July 2011

ISBN: 978-0-9832592-0-6

Part IV contains a revised version of Parts I-VI of *Problem Solvers and Soul Winners: A Handbook for Deacons and Deaconesses*, AVA's Book Publishers, 1999.

Contents

Therefore, brethren, pick out from among you seven men of good repute, full of the Spirit and of wisdom, whom we may appoint to this duty. But we will devote ourselves to prayer and to the ministry of the word. And the word of God increased; and the number of the disciples multiplied in Jerusalem greatly.

Acts 6:3-4, 7 (RSV)

I commend to you our sister Phoebe, a deaconess of the church at Cenchreae, that you may receive her in whatever she may require from you, for she has been a helper of many and of myself as well.

Rom 16:1-2 (RSV)

Foreword

More than a trite saying is the consideration that "timing is everything." These words find a secure place in the realm of reality as congregations and church leaders rejoice when they become aware of practical resources that assist in meeting the ministry need at seemingly just the right moment.

Such will be the experience of those pastors and congregational leaders that are in search of biblical, historical, practical, and methodical means of facilitating movement in their deacons and deaconesses from a service mindset that primarily involves offering collection, building maintenance, baptism and Holy Communion preparation, and other ceremonial appearances.

This volume, *The Twenty-First Century Deacon and Deaconess: Reflecting the Biblical Model*, by Dr. Vincent E. White, Sr., is a positive and powerful addition to the all-too-limited cadre of volumes that are dedicated to assisting the deacon and deaconess in the process of functioning within the realm of a Holy Ghost anointed ministry.

The Twenty-First Century Deacon and Deaconess is a detailed handbook and guide that provides structure, affirmation, instruction, and encouragement. It challenges the status-quo and identifies the underlying factors that reveal that the under-utilization of deacons and deaconesses in the Seventh-day Adventist church is a systemic problem. It also offers recommendations for addressing this problem in such a way that these officers can be restored to their biblically defined roles. The book reaches while maintaining balance, as it views the landscape of this powerful ministry that is designed to assist in the process of congregational nurture and growth.

Local congregations will benefit from the exercise they receive as they journey through this very timely and straight forward call to excellence in the ministry of deacons and deaconesses. The Seventh-day Adventist church at large will benefit from accepting the challenge to embrace a paradigm shift that would better equip these officers to assist in fulfilling the church's mission to spread the gospel to the world. The result of such a shift would be, as it was in the first century Christian church when the seven deacons were elected to serve—"The Word of God increased; and the number of the disciples multiplied . . ." (Acts 6:7).

Without reservations, I highly recommend this book. It is a "must-have" for deacons, deaconesses, pastors, and church administrators.

J. Alfred Johnson, II
Director of Adult Ministries
The Seventh-day Adventist Church
in North America

Acknowledgments

Special thanks to Elder J. Alfred Johnson, II, Director of Adult Ministries of the Seventh-day Adventist Church in North America, for writing the foreword to this book, and for the way in which he and Paula have modeled humility to Audrey and me over the years.

Thanks to Kenley D. Hall, D.Min., who served as my doctoral dissertation adviser, for the guidance and encouragement he gave me. Thanks also to the other members of the Andrews University Doctor of Ministry Dissertation Defense Committee—Trevor O'Reggio, Ph.D., Skip Bell, D.Min., and Martin Hannah, Ph.D.— for challenging me to be a voice for deacons and deaconesses by placing my research in public view so that dialogue for change may occur. The writing of this book is a step toward meeting that challenge.

I am grateful for the mentoring of the deceased (2004) Elder Eric C. Ward, former pastor of the Oakwood College (now University) Seventh-day Adventist Church, Huntsville, Alabama. When I was a student at Oakwood, I was privileged to assist him. It was there that I grew to respect and appreciate the sacred work of deacons and deaconesses.

Thanks to Elder Steven Norman, Communication Secretary of the Southern Union Conference of Seventh-day Adventists, for recommending me to conduct a training seminar for the deacons and deaconesses of our conference in January 1999. It was that event that challenged me to study the work of these officers.

Thanks to all of the pastors, deacons, and deaconesses who have purchased my first book, *Problem Solvers and Soul Winners: A Handbook for Deacons and Deaconesses*, 1999, and have invited me to conduct training seminars at their churches.

Thanks to my friends and colleagues Elders Wayne Martin (Jean) and Llewellyn Williams (Cynthia) for their support and encouragement through the years. They are two of the original members of the Forty-Seven Club.

Finally, special thanks to my wife, Audrey—my main source of encouragement and support; a wonderful Christian, mother, and friend. To my son, Dr. Vincent E. White, Jr., DC, and daughter, Angella V. White. I am very proud of both of them. Angella served as proofreader of this book, and Shalanda Edwards-White, my daughter-in-law, served as graphic designer.

PART I

Toward a Theology of Ministry for Deacons and Deaconesses

Introduction

The ministry of Jesus as a servant provides the foundation for a theology of ministry for deacons and deaconesses. Jesus defined His ministry in terms of service by stating that He "came not to be ministered unto, but to minister" (Matt 20:28). The Greek words for "to be ministered unto" (διακονηθῆναι) and "to minister" (διακονῆσαι) come from the root word διακονέω which is derived from the word διάκονος (deacon). This implies that deacons and deaconesses are people whose ministry is to render service to others. They are called to follow the example of Jesus, who, in His earthly ministry, was the "Deacon" par excellence.

There are wider implications that can be drawn from the ministry of deacons and deaconesses for the church at large. Deacons and deaconesses symbolize the work of the church. Therefore, every church member is a deacon or deaconess although he or she may not bear the title. Jesus calls everyone who becomes a member of His church to a ministry of service.

The deacons of the first century Christian church were elected based upon spiritual qualifications—an "honest report, full of the Holy Ghost and wisdom" (Acts 6:3). These qualifications enabled them to carry out their responsibilities of solving relational problems among the members, caring for the needs of the poor, and teaching the Word of God. Scriptural evidence and extra-biblical sources indicate that female deacons or deaconesses served the first century Christian church. They ministered to the women, especially to those who were poor and sick. Deaconesses have continued to serve in various church denominations throughout the centuries.

Although very little is written about the work of deacons and deaconesses in the early history of the Seventh-day Adventist church, these officers did exist, and still do. The church has always recognized and embraced the theological grounds for their ministry. However, the major challenge is that the other departments that the Seventh-day Adventist church has created are carrying out many of the responsibilities that the deacons and deaconesses did in the first century Christian church. Therefore, these officers are under-utilized today. Part I consists of the following chapters:

CHAPTER 1

Jesus' Model of Servant Ministry

The Old Testament prophet Isaiah, when writing about the first advent of Jesus, described His life's ministry as a servant. In Isa 61:1-2, he identified Jesus' ministry as a servant to the meek, broken-hearted, captives, and those that mourn. In Isa 53:11, God, through the prophet, referred to Jesus as "my righteous servant [who will] justify many; for he shall bear their iniquity." Throughout His life on earth, Jesus fulfilled these prophecies concerning Himself. He ministered to the spiritual, physical, and emotional needs of those He came in contact with. Most of Jesus' ministry was devoted to nurturing and training His disciples and healing the sick. Ellen G. White stated,

> During His ministry, Jesus devoted more time to healing the sick than to preaching. His miracles testified to the truth of His words, that He came not to destroy, but to save. The Saviour made each work of healing an occasion for implanting divine principles in the mind and soul. This was the purpose of His work. He imparted earthly blessings, that He might incline the hearts of men to receive the gospel of His grace.[1]

As Jesus went about healing the afflicted and preaching the gospel, He took His disciples along with Him. This was His method of training them for their future work of ministry. As their faith in Him increased and they learned to follow His instructions, He sent them out to do as they had seen Him do. Upon returning from one assignment that He sent them on, they rejoiced that they had accomplished the same results that they had seen Him accomplish—devils were subjected to them through His name. His response to them was, "Notwithstanding in this rejoice not, that the spirits are

---

[1]Ellen G. White, *The Ministry of Healing* (1905; repr., Nampa, ID: Pacific Press, 1942), 19-20.

subject unto you; but rather rejoice, because your names are written in heaven" (Luke 10:17, 20).

There was an important lesson for His disciples to learn in this response. Jesus wanted them to recognize the self-destructive danger that comes with the love for power. Commenting on this text, Ellen White stated, "Rejoice not in the possession of power, lest you lose sight of your dependence upon God. Be careful lest self-sufficiency come in, and you work in your own strength, rather than in the spirit and strength of your Master. Self is ever ready to take the credit if any measure of success attends the work."[2]

The concept that Jesus was trying to instill in His disciples was that ministry is not about power, control, and greatness as viewed by worldly standards, but it is about service to God and humanity. He stated this principle succinctly on the occasion when His disciples were jockeying for positions of power in His kingdom. He said, "Ye know that the princes of the Gentiles exercise dominion over them, and they that are great exercise authority upon them. But it shall not be so among you: but whosoever will be great among you, let him be your minister; And whosoever will be chief among you, let him be your servant: Even as the Son of man came not to be ministered unto, but to minister, and to give his life a ransom for many" (Matt 20:25-28).

Here, Jesus indicated that His life's mission was to serve others rather than being served Himself. This was His model for ministry. The Greek words for "to be ministered unto" (διακονηθῆναι) and "to minister" (διακονῆσαι) come from the root word διακονέω which is derived from the word διάκονος (deacon)—masculine and feminine. It is when the article is used with the word that the gender distinction is made—ὁ διάκονος (masculine), ἡ διάκονος (feminine). The word for deacon (διάκονος) means "one who renders service to another; an attendant, servant."[3]

D. Edmond Hiebert, commenting on the above passage of Scripture, says,

---

[2]Ellen G. White, *The Desire of Ages* (1898; repr., Mountain View, CA: Pacific Press, 1940), 493.

[3]Harold K. Moulton, ed., *The Analytical Greek Lexicon*, rev. ed. (1978), s.v. "διάκονος."

Jesus taught that believers must voluntarily serve other believers, motivated and inspired by His own example of service (Matt. 20:26-28; Mark 10:45). The terms thus came to denote loving service to brothers and neighbors, which is to be the distinguishing mark of Christ's followers. Jesus taught His disciples that instead of lording it over others, they must be willing to serve others (Matt. 20:25-26). Such service was a way to greatness among them, 'Whoever wishes to become great among you shall be your servant' (διάκονος; Matt. 20:26). Those who aspire to be leaders must voluntarily stoop to serve.[4]

Henry Webb states,

> The primary model for all Christians is Jesus Christ himself. He "left you an example, so that you would follow in his steps" (1 Peter 2:21, GNB). Jesus came to serve.
> All Jesus' followers were to serve by providing ministry in his name. The title diakonos (servant) applied to every Christian, but the apostle Paul also used it in a special sense for specific church leaders (Phil. 1:1; 1 Tim. 3). Translators chose not to translate literally in those situations but to make a new English word deacon out of the Greek word for servant. Thus deacons carry both the name of Christ and the name of servant.[5]

Ellen White shared this insight on Jesus' life as a servant. She said,

> Among His disciples Christ was in every sense a caretaker, a burden bearer. He shared their poverty, He practiced self-denial on their account, He went before them to smooth the more difficult places, and soon He would consummate His work on earth by laying down His life. The principle on

---

[4]D. Edmond Hiebert, "Behind the Word 'Deacon': A New Testament Study," *Bibliotheca Sacra* 140 (April-June 1983): 157.

[5]Henry Webb, *Deacons: Servant Models in the Church* (Nashville: Convention Press, 1980), 11-12.

which Christ acted is to actuate the members of the church which is His body.[6]

Herein lies the connection of the life ministry of Jesus as a servant with all who have determined to follow Him. He has called them to a self-denying ministry of service. Therefore, the challenge that He presented to His followers when He was here on earth is applicable to His present day followers. The challenge is, "If any man will come after me, let him deny himself, and take up his cross, and follow me" (Matt 16:24).

Hiebert states that "in His earthly ministry Jesus Himself was the 'Deacon' par excellence. He set the example not only for deacons but for all believers."[7] James Monroe Barnett likens the deacon as a symbol of the church's ministry. He says,

> The origin of diaconate and its development in the first centuries reveals above all the deacon as symbol. He is the symbol par excellence of the Church's ministry. In the deacon is seen the indelible character of service Christ put on his ministry and of servant on those who minister. He is the embodiment of the first principle of this ministry which is sent to serve.[8]

Therefore, it is evident that Jesus' ministry as a servant provides the theological foundation for the ministry of deacon and deaconess. As deacons and deaconesses follow Jesus' example, they are to enlist the members of the church into a life of service.

---

[6]Ellen White, *The Desire of Ages*, 550.

[7]Hiebert, 160.

[8]James Monroe Barnett, *The Diaconate---A Full and Equal Order: A Comprehensive and Critical Study of the Origin, Development, and Decline of the Diaconate in the Context of the Church's Total Ministry and a Proposal for Renewal* (New York: Seabury Press, 1981), 141.

CHAPTER 2

The Role of Deacons
in the First Century Christian Church

The biblical account of the selection of deacons in the first century Christian church is recorded in Acts 6:1-8:

> And in those days, when the number of the disciples was multiplied, there arose a murmuring of the Grecians against the Hebrews, because their widows were neglected in the daily ministration. Then the twelve called the multitude of the disciples unto them, and said, It is not reason that we should leave the word of God, and serve tables. Wherefore, brethren, look ye out among you seven men of honest report, full of the Holy Ghost and wisdom, whom we may appoint over this business. But we will give ourselves continually to prayer, and to the ministry of the word. And the saying pleased the whole multitude: and they chose Stephen, a man full of faith and the Holy Ghost, and Philip and Prochorus, and Nicanor, and Timon, and Parmenas, and Nicolas a proselyte of Antioch: whom they set before the apostles: and when they had prayed, they laid their hands on them. And the word of God increased; and the number of the disciples multiplied in Jerusalem greatly; and a great company of the priests were obedient to the faith. And Stephen, full of faith and power, did great wonders and miracles among the people.

Ellen White gave the background surrounding the selection of these deacons. She stated that "the early church was made up of many classes of people, of various nationalities."[9] This was due to the converting power of the Holy Spirit on the Day of Pentecost. Acts 2 informs us that the Holy Spirit fell upon many of the dispersed Jews

---

[9]Ellen White, *The Acts of the Apostles* (Boise, ID: Pacific Press, 1911), 87.

of every nation that had gathered at Jerusalem for this feast day. Among that group, were those commonly known as Grecians or Hellenistic Jews. There was a division between the Grecian Jews and the Palestinian Jews. They were divided by their language and culture. One group spoke Greek and grew up absorbed by the Greek culture. The other group spoke Hebrew or Aramaic and grew up in Palestine. Despite the existing differences of these two groups, the Holy Spirit brought them together in harmony and in love. They were of one accord and had all things in common. They sold what they had and divided it among themselves. They visited each other daily and ate together with gladness and singleness of heart (Acts 2:1, 44-46).

The unity of spirit was short-lived as old prejudices of the past resurfaced. Feelings of distrust, jealousy, and suspicion brought about faultfinding and murmuring. Allegations were made that the Grecian widows were being neglected in the "daily ministration."[10] The RSV translation calls it the "daily distribution" (Acts 6:1). Ellen White referred to it as the "daily distribution of assistance."[11] However, the Greek word for "ministration" is διακονία. This is the office and the work of a διάκονος (deacon).

As previously stated, these words describe the life ministry of Jesus, according to Matt 20:28. It is from these words that we get the word deacon, which means to minister or to serve. Webb observes:

> English Bibles usually translate the Greek word diakonos as "servant" or "minister." However in Philippians 1:1 and 1 Timothy 3:8-13 the translators created from the Greek word diakonos a new English word, deacon. These passages seem to refer to specific church leaders or officers who were closely linked with bishops (pastors). Apparently, as the number of believers increased and new churches were begun, the congregations formalized the servant role into a more specific church office. The high qualifications for deacons

---

[10]Vincent E. White, Sr., *Problem Solvers and Soul Winners: A Handbook for Deacons and Deaconesses* (Huntsville, AL: AVA's Book Publishers, 1999), xvi-xvii.

[11]Ellen White, *The Acts of the Apostles*, 88.

indicate that the New Testament congregations looked to these church leaders as examples in ministry to persons.[12]

Kenneth D. Catoe states that "diakonos literally means 'through dust.' Although the origin of the word is questioned, the concept of raising dust suggests a servant hastening to serve or to wait on his master."[13] Hiebert also mentions this questionable origin of the word; but adds, "More probably the verbal root was διήκω, 'to reach from one place to another,' akin to the verb διώκω, 'to hasten after, to pursue.' Then the root idea is one who reaches out with diligence and persistence to render a service on behalf of others. This would imply that the deacon reaches out to render love-prompted service to others energetically and persistently."[14]

Therefore, as we trace the roots of the office of deacons, we discover that the reason that they came into existence was to serve and to share the responsibilities of the work. They came into existence because of a problem. Therefore, the primary function of the first century deacons was to solve problems that arose in the church. The *SDA Bible Commentary* gives this description of the problem of taking care of the poor:

> Since there were no church buildings in that early day, nor indeed until nearly two centuries later, and since no money was needed yet for the salaries of ministers or the dispatching of missionaries, the funds donated were used for the support of the poor and needy. In any large congregation of five thousand to ten thousand, there would ordinarily be a large number of such members. But the transitional difficulty of entering the Christian fellowship, in a city as prejudiced against the Nazarene as Jerusalem was at that time, must have meant to many a dislocation in employment and serious social and economic disabilities. Doubtless the seven men

---

[12]Webb, *Deacons: Servant Models in the* Church, 74-75.

[13]Kenneth D. Catoe, "Equipping Deacons for Ministry" (D.Min. dissertation, Drew University, 1989), 13.

[14]Hiebert, 153.

had much work to do in taking care of the needs of the poor and the deprived in the congregations.[15]

David S. Dockery further describes this problem by saying,

> A feature of early church life was readiness to meet the needs of the poor. The growth of the church, however, prevented this ministry from being carried out as well as it should have been. It was inevitable that with the development of different groups in the church and the difficulty of ongoing communication between these groups, someone would be overlooked.[16]

The deacons of the early church were not simply ordinary men, because the church was not confronted with an ordinary problem. The murmuring of the Grecians against the Hebrews over the distribution of assistance was simply the presenting or surface problem, which was symptomatic of a larger spiritual problem that was even greater than their cultural differences.[17] Ellen White described the problem as follows: "The enemy [Satan] succeeded in arousing the suspicions of some who had formerly been in the habit of looking with jealousy on their brethren in the faith and of finding fault with their spiritual leaders."[18] From this, it can be concluded that Satan had launched a spiritual attack against the church in an attempt to hinder it from growing and ultimately to destroy it. "Therefore, the church needed men 'of honest report, full of the Holy Ghost and wisdom' (Acts 6:3) to look beyond the symptoms and see the real issues, then bring about resolution."[19]

---

[15]"The Deaconate," *SDA Bible Commentary*, ed. Francis D. Nichol (1956; repr., Washington, DC: Review and Herald Pub. Assn., 1980), 6:25.

[16]David S. Dockery, "Acts 6-12: The Christian Mission Beyond Jerusalem," *Review and Exposition* 87 (Summer 1990): 423-424.

[17]Vincent White, xvii-xviii.

[18]Ellen White, *The Acts of the Apostles*, 88.

[19]Vincent White, xviii.

The spiritual qualities required of the deacons of the first century Christian church strongly imply that their calling was a spiritual calling, and their responsibilities were far greater than just waiting on tables. Nancy Vyhmeister suggests, "Theirs was evidently a spiritual occupation, for the requirements were spiritual, personal integrity, and blamelessness."[20]

Although the evidence is clear enough for me to support the idea that the seven men selected in Acts 6 were deacons, others have suggested that they were not. Barnett presents this argument:

> Further, the Seven are not called "deacons" here or elsewhere in the New Testament, and it is almost certain that they did not hold that office. Their office was unique and was not continued in the Church. The word "deacon" is, in fact, never used in Acts. André Lemaire in reviewing recent research on ministries in the New Testament reports that the majority of scholars support this conclusion: the Seven were not deacons. Irenaeus (c. 185) was the first of the early Church fathers to call the Seven deacons.[21]

Edward P. Echlin further adds: "Another reason for caution in referring to the seven as "deacons" in the clearly defined meaning of that office is that Stephen and Philip continued to preach and baptize, functions customarily performed at that time by the apostles and presbyters (Acts 6:8; 8:5)."[22]

However, Harold Nichols' view is not in opposition with Ellen G. White, as is Barnett and Echlin. He states:

> It must be pointed out that the seven men chosen for the special tasks of caring for the widows and serving tables were not specifically called deacons in Acts 6. First, and foremost,

---

[20]Nancy Vyhmeister, "The Ministry of the Deaconess Through History," *Ministry*, July 2008, 17.

[21]Barnett, 30.

[22]Edward P. Echlin, *The Deacon in the Church: Past Time and Future* (Staten Island, NY: Alba House, 1971), 8.

they were called to perform a service. When the term "deacon" is used subsequently in the New Testament, it is generally assumed that it refers to men who were performing service similar to that which was assigned to the original seven who were selected. This assumption seems logical when it is understood that the Greek word from which "deacon" is derived usually describes the work of a servant. Whether or not there was a difference between the tasks described in the Book of Acts and that which might be called the office of deacon in the church seems today to be inconsequential. The fact is that these people performed the work of serving; therefore they may be called deacons, or those who serve.[23]

---

[23]Harold Nichols, *The Work of the Deacon and Deaconess* (Valley Forge, PA: Judson Press, 1964), 1-2.

CHAPTER 3

Female Deacons of the
First Century Christian Church

Although 1 Tim 3 provides undisputed evidence for the office of bishop and deacon, there are those who believe that verse 11 supports the existence of female deacons or deaconesses in the first century Christian church. Vyhmeister is a proponent of this view. The text states, "Even so must their wives be grave, not slanderers, sober, faithful in all things" (1 Tim 3:11). Vyhmeister states,

> The Greek word, which can be translated "women" or "wives," has been variously translated as "women," "women deacons," or "their [deacon's] wives."
>
> The suggestion that the term refers to wives of deacons presents difficulties, for in the Greek there is no possessive. Whose wives were they? On the other hand, if one takes the context seriously, these women serve the church as do their male counterparts. Quite probably, these women were female deacons, as was Phoebe.
>
> In the late second century, Clement of Alexandria (155-220) indicated that this text presented evidence for the existence of diakonon gunaikōn ("women deacons"). John Chrysostom and Theodoret, writing in the fourth and fifth centuries respectively, also understood these women to be female deacons.[24]

Vyhmeister is correct in her observation that there is no possessive in the Greek construct of this text. The word γυναῖκας, translated as "women," is in the accusative case and not in the genitive case, which is possessive.[25]

---

[24]Vyhmeister, "The Ministry of the Deaconess," 18.

[25]Moulton, s.v. "γυναῖκας."

Shirley A. Groh also believes that these women were deaconesses. She states, "In I Timothy 3:8 ff. Paul speaks of the duties of a deacon. Then in v. 11 he says, 'The women likewise must be serious, no slanderer, but temperate, faithful in all things.' R.S.V. Many believe this refers especially to Deaconesses. They were to be cultured and devoted women."[26]

Robert M. Lewis agrees that the Greek word for "wives" can be variously translated—"wives," "widow," "bride," or "any adult woman" (married or unmarried),[27] but he disagrees that these women are deaconesses. He suggests that the women of 1 Tim 3:11 are not "a select group of women known as 'deaconesses' which many consider to be a third office of the church [neither are they] . . . the wives of those men who are deacons and should reflect their husband's godly character."[28] They are "unmarried women committed unconditionally to the service of the church and who in meeting certain character qualities, have been enlisted to aid the deacons in the outworking of their office."[29]

Lewis further argues that if these women were limited to being the wives of deacons, those wives that could not assist their husbands because of large family responsibilities would cause their husbands to be disqualified to serve as deacons. Lewis points out that because married women's ministry is centered in the home (1 Tim 2:9-15; 5:8, 14, 16; 2 Tim 3:14-15; Titus 2:3-5), whether they are married to a deacon or any man, the women mentioned in this passage are unmarried.

Lewis' final argument is that, "with the detailed qualifications for both elder and deacon so plainly spelled out, why a parenthesizing of the deacons' female counterpart? If these women held a full third

---

[26]Shirley A. Groh, "The Role of Deaconess Through the Ages," December 1955, http://www.wlsessays.net/GrohRole.pdf (accessed October 13, 2008).

[27]Robert M. Lewis, "The 'Women' of 1 Timothy 3:11," *Bibliotheca Sacra* 136 (April-June 1979): 168.

[28]Ibid., 167.

[29]Ibid., 175.

office of the church, why do they not merit a paragraph of their own?"[30]

Although Lewis presents an interesting case, however, taking the context seriously as Vyhmeister suggests, I concur with Vyhmeister that these women were female deacons. As to Lewis' argument that if these women were female deacons/deaconesses, they would have merited a paragraph of their own, my response is that the male dominate society in which they lived seldom gave women the recognition that they merited. Therefore, to parenthesize what was expected of them was not unusual behavior.

It is probable that most of the first century deaconesses were unmarried or widows. Citing the *Apostolic Constitutions*, Groh says that "a deaconess shall be 'a pure virgin' or 'a widow once married, faithful and worthy.' This is natural since family cares prevent full concentration on the job of Deaconess, and in the 2nd century A.D. this was no small job."[31]

Although the ideal was that deaconesses be unmarried, there were exceptions to this. Philip Schaff states that Prisca (Priscilla) probably served as a deaconess.[32] She was married to Aquila. She assisted him in their tent making business, traveling with the apostle Paul, and teaching God's Word (Acts 18:1-3, 18, 24-26). She had the ability to perform multiple tasks, and Paul did not limit her. Paul presents singleness as the ideal status for both men and women that do the Lord's work. This is because of the distractions that are associated with marriage. However, Paul recognized that there are those that need to be married, and he did not restrict their involvement in the Lord's work (1 Cor 7:32-40). Therefore, married women who desire to serve as deaconesses today are not to be excluded. They must, however, seek God's guidance on how to balance the demands of the home with the responsibilities of this office.

There are also other Scriptures that indicate that female deacons or deaconesses existed in the first century Christian church. In Rom

---

[30]Ibid., 171-172.

[31]Groh.

[32]Philip Schaff, *Apostolic Chrisitianity (A.D. 1-100)*, vol. 1 of *History of the Christian Church* (1910; repr., Grand Rapids: Wm. B. Eerdmans Publishing Company, 1985), 500-501.

16:1-2, the apostle Paul stated, "I commend unto you Phebe our sister, which is a servant of the church which is at Cenchrea: That ye receive her in the Lord, as becometh saints, and that ye assist her in whatsoever business she hath need of you: for she hath been a succourer of many, and of myself also." Note that the name is spelled "Phoebe" by most sources. However, it is spelled "Phebe" in the *KJV*.

The Greek word διάκονον used in this Scripture is the accusative case (the object of a verb) of διάκονος, and is translated in English as "deacon or deaconess, whose official duty was to superintend the alms of the Church, with other kindred services."[33] The *SDA Bible Commentary* states that "the use of this term suggests that the office of 'deaconess' may already have been established in the early Christian church. At least Phoebe was in some sense a servant or minister in the congregation at Cenchreae."[34] Vhymeister states that "Theodoret (393-460) noted Phoebe as 'a woman deacon, prominent and noble. She was so rich in good works performed as to have merited the praise of Paul.'"[35] Paul described Phoebe as "a succourer of many." According to Maurice Riley this means "a helper of many (one who shields from suffering, goes out to the aid of one in distress)."[36] Groh likens the role that Phoebe played as a succourer to today's social worker. She says, "We note that her [Phoebe] work as a 'helper' or 'Succourer' of many both spiritually and physically, no doubt ran much in the path of a social worker of today, of course the religious motivation made her office primarily one of the church, but it was felt also in the social order of things."[37]

Nichols concurs with the idea that deaconesses were present in the first century Christian church. He says,

---

[33]Moulton, s.v. "διάκονος," "διάκονον."

[34]"Servant," *SDA Bible Commentary*, 6:649.

[35]Vyhmeister, "The Ministry of the Deaconess," 18.

[36]Maurice Riley, *The Deaconess: Walking in the Newness of Life*, 2nd ed. (Newark, NJ: Christian Associates Publications, 1993), 1.

[37]Groh.

In the New Testament church, when seven individuals were chosen to minister to widows and serve tables, all of them were men (cf. Acts 6:1-6). Nevertheless, the New Testament does record the presence of women workers in the churches. Paul wrote to the church at Philippi: "Help these women, for they have labored side by side with me in the gospel. . ." (Phil. 4:3). In the letter to the Romans Paul wrote: "I commend to you our sister Phoebe, a deaconess of the church at Cenchreae, that you may . . . help her in whatever she may require of you, for she has been a helper of many and of myself as well" (Rom. 16:1-2). These references imply that many, if not all, early churches had in them women who served and were called deaconesses.[38]

Philip Schaff states that "Paul mentions Phoebe as a deaconess of the church of Cenchreae, the port of Corinth, and it is more than probable that Prisca (Priscilla), Mary, Tryphaena, Tryphosa, and Persis, whom he commends for their labor in the Lord, served in the same capacity at Rome."[39]

Schaff also indicates that "deaconesses, or female helpers, had a similar charge of the poor and sick in the female portion of the church. This office was the more needful on account of the rigid separation of the sexes at that day, especially among the Greeks and Orientals."[40]

Groh gives this vivid picture of the deaconesses' caring for the sick:

> When we stop to remember that there were no hospitals, we can begin to imagine what a big job is implied even in the words saying that the deaconess "administered to the poor and sick." No provisions were made for the sick except by this one woman worker. Imagine even a small out-break of flu with only deaconesses to administer help and probably care for sick mothers' families yet, too. This is a full time job.

---

[38]Nichols, 86-87.

[39]Schaff, 1:500-501.

[40]Ibid., 500.

People's physical surroundings had to be set in order that Christ might better work in their hearts. In addition to this social work and nursing, the deaconess had the more strictly religious duties of teaching, doorkeeping, and assisting at baptisms. Here was no small task, and it required, as one author said, 'A gifted individual with personal endowments of a religious kind' plus much courage to perform all these tasks.[41]

Riley further substantiates the existence of deaconesses in the early church. She states that,

> Many if not all, early Christian churches had women, who served as, and were called deaconesses. During the first five Christian centuries, some of the help rendered by the deaconess was to assist the presbyter in the baptism of women: greet the women parishioners, direct them to their seats, and maintain order among them. This was according to a document called the apostolic constitution in church discipline, doctrine, and worship. It also stipulated that deaconesses were to be ordained for the ministrations toward women. She was referred to as the assistant to the deacon, and was to be present at all interviews between women and the priest, bishop or deacon.[42]

In addition to declaring that deaconesses existed in the early Christian church, Riley also states that they were ordained to carry out their ministry. Charles W. Deweese makes this observation concerning their ordination:

> Deaconesses were evidently not ordained in the first three centuries. Such ordination, whenever it began, was an eastern custom, for churches in the West did not ordain women. A fourth-century eastern writing presented a suggested procedure for ordaining a deaconess. After she passed a

---

[41]Groh.

[42]Riley, 1.

careful preliminary examination, the bishop was to lay hands upon her in the presence of the presbyters, deacons, and other deaconesses. The bishop then ended the service with an ordination prayer.[43]

Schaff recorded the prayer, taken from the *Apostolic Constitutions* (late fourth century),

> Eternal God, Father of our Lord Jesus Christ, Creator of man and woman, who didst fill Miriam and Deborah and Hannah and Huldah with the Spirit, and didst not disdain to suffer thine only-begotten Son to be born of a woman; who also in the tabernacle and the temple didst appoint women keepers of thine holy gates: look down now upon this thine handmaid, who is designated to the office of deacon, and grant her the Holy Ghost, and cleanse her from all filthiness of the flesh and of the spirit, that she may worthily execute the work intrusted to her, to thine honor and to the praise of thine Anointed; to whom with thee and the Holy Ghost be honor and adoration forever. Amen.[44]

Riley, likening deaconesses to "Angels of Mercy," refers to Phoebe and Dorcas as biblical examples of such.[45] Luke gives us the account of Dorcas in the Book of Acts. "Now there was at Joppa a certain disciple named Tabitha, which by interpretation is called Dorcas: this woman was full of good works and almsdeeds which she did. When he [Peter] was come all the widows stood by him weeping, and shewing the coats and garments which Dorcas made, while she was with them" (Acts 9:36, 39). Like Phoebe, Tabitha was a succourer—a helper, a protector, one who shields from suffering, and goes out to the aid of those in distress. She showed compassion for

---

[43]Charles W. Deweese, *The Emerging Role of Deacons* (Nashville: Broadman Press, 1979), 15-16.

[44]Philip Schaff, *Nicene and Post-Nicene Christianity (A.D. 311-600)*, vol. 3 of *History of the Christian Church*, 260.

[45]Riley, 33.

the underprivileged of Joppa, and made coats and garments to protect them from the weather.

CHAPTER 4

Deacons and Deaconesses
in Early Adventism

Research from the Ellen G. White Writings Complete Published Edition 2005 revealed that of the fifteen times that the word deacon(s) was used; only four occurrences relate to their ministry in the early Seventh-day Adventist church. Of the eighteen times that the word deaconess(es) was used, only three relate to their ministry in the early Seventh-day Adventist church.

The first area concerning the deacons pertained to the kind of wine that they should use in the ordinance of Holy Communion. The following statement is a critique of the book *Prophetess of Health* that was published in the *Review and Herald* 29:222, April 16, 1867. The issue was what did Ellen White mean when she said that she approved of a "little domestic wine." Here is the response,

> Domestic wine occasionally referred to by Ellen White and in the Review and Herald, we would understand to be the juice of the grape pressed out and at first free from fermentation. It must be remembered that in 1867, 1868 and 1869 there was no sure and effective method of preserving grape juice unfermented. This meant that even utilizing the best means available for preserving grape juice, it would eventually gain an alcoholic content. Concerning the use of this kind of wine in the ordinances, James White counseled in 1867: "Know what you use. Let the deacons obtain the cultivated grape, see the wine made, and secure from the air to keep it from fermenting as much as possible."[46]

This statement indicates that the deacons in the early Seventh-day Adventist church were responsible for supplying the wine used in the

---

[46]*Ellen G. White Writings*, Complete Published Edition 2005, Ellen G. White Estate Research Documents Full Text Search, s.v. "deacons" [CD-ROM] (Silver Spring, MD: Ellen G. White Estate, 2006).

ordinance of Holy Communion. In that they were instructed to use unfermented grape juice for this ordinance, may also imply that they were required to abstain from fermented wine, as were the deacons of the first century Christian church, according to 1 Tim 3:8—"Be not addicted to much wine." However, it is not clear from the above statement if the deacons in the early Seventh-day Adventist church also participated in serving the emblems—wine and bread—at the Holy Communion services.

The second area relating to the deacons' ministry in the early Seventh-day Adventist church pertained to their responsibility in handling the tithe. In the following letter, the issue was that the Battle Creek church needed additional persons—a clerk and a treasurer—other than the deacons to look after the tithe. Ellen White agreed with the Battle Creek church's decision to use a portion of their tithes to pay their clerk and treasurer for the service they rendered. That practice was also adopted by other large churches. The St. Helena Sanitarium church paid its treasurer. The treasurer was also referred to as a tithe collector. C. F. McVagh, president of the Southern Union Conference, wrote a letter to W. C. White on October 24, 1912 to get verification that Ellen White approved of this practice. W. C. White's response was,

> In the olden days, when the Battle Creek church was growing, it was found that unless the work of collecting the tithe was followed up regularly that the amount received was very much less than if the matter were followed up in a businesslike way by a collector who made the work his regular duty. We also found that this work demanded more time than it was right for us to ask any one, two, or three of the deacons to give to the matter, and it was thought by the church council that it would be good policy, and for the best interests of the tithe payers, and for the best interests of the conference, to have a good collector chosen and employed and paid a reasonable amount for his time. This plan, with the reasons therefore, was placed before Father and Mother, and received their hearty approval.[47]

---

[47]Ibid.

This next statement also dealt with the responsibility of the deacons in relationship to the tithe. The purpose of this statement was to clarify where the storehouse is.

> A fair reading of Ellen White's statement leads un-questionably to the conclusion that, in her mind, the church treasury was the store house of Malachi 3. She used the words "treasury" and "storehouse" as synonyms when she wrote, "If all the tithes were brought into the storehouse, God's treasury would not be empty." Concerning the church treasury, she stated: "Many presidents of state conferences do not attend to that which is their work–to see that the elders and deacons of the churches do their work in the churches, by seeing that a faithful tithe is brought into the treasury."[48]

It can be concluded from these two sources, that the deacons in the early Seventh-day Adventist church were responsible for collecting the tithe from the members. Sometime before the death of James White in 1881, after the deacons collected the tithe in the larger churches, specifically at Battle Creek, they turned the tithe over to the treasurer or tithe collector of the church. However, according to the letter W. C. White wrote to C. F. McVagh, the smaller churches did not follow the practice of hiring a treasurer. Therefore, the implication is that the deacons collected the tithe and served as treasurer in the smaller churches.

Finally, the third area relating to the deacons' ministry in the early Seventh-day Adventist church pertained to their ordination. The following statement by Arthur N. Patrick, who was the registrar at Avondale College in Australia, indicates that both deacons and deaconesses were ordained in the early Seventh-day Adventist church.

> June 24, 1899, the Ashfield church in Sydney elected G. F. Goodman as elder. The church records tell us that he "was ordained as elder by the laying on of hands." Clearly, Adventists at the time understood the laying on of hands as effecting ordination.

---

[48]Ibid.

Which officers were ordained to their tasks? Again the Ashfield church minutes, in two separate entries, give us the answer. At the meeting on August 10, 1895, the nominating committee rendered its report. The record notes: "immediately following the election, the officers were called to the front, where Pastors Corliss and McCullagh set apart the elder, deacons, [and] deaconesses by prayer and the laying on of hands."

On Sabbath, January 6, 1900, Elder W. C. White presided over the regular Sabbath meeting at Ashfield. The clerk's minutes note: "The previous Sabbath officers had been nominated and accepted for the current year, and today Elder White ordained and laid hands on the elders, deacon, and deaconesses."

The page from W. C. White's diary for this date confirms the Ashfield church's records: "Spoke at Ashfield. Twenty-five present. Ordained J. Hindson Elder, Thos. Patchin Deacon, and Mrs. Brannyrane and Patchin Deaconesses."[49]

It is clear from this letter and the record of the church's minutes that both deacons and deaconesses were ordained in the early Seventh-day Adventist church.

In addition to these two instances where deaconesses were ordained, Vyhmeister, documents two more occasions—one in February or March 1916, when E. E. Andross, then president of the Pacific Union Conference, officiated the service; and in 1921 at a church in Sarawak (Malaysia) where F. A. Detamore witnessed the ordination of a Sister Lee.[50]

The second and final area relating to the deaconesses' ministry in the early Seventh-day Adventist church described some of the duties that they performed. Ellen White gave this brief description of their work, as well as recommended that they be ordained, in an article she wrote in the *Review and Herald*, July 9, 1895. She stated,

---

[49]Ibid.

[50]Nancy Vyhmeister, "Deaconesses in the Church," *Ministry*, September 2008, 23

Women who are willing to consecrate some of their time to the service of the Lord should be appointed to visit the sick, look after the young, and minister to the necessities of the poor. They should be set apart to this work by prayer and laying on of hands. In some cases they will need to counsel with the church officers or the ministers; but if they are devoted women, maintaining a vital connection with God, they will be a power for good in the church. This is another means of strengthening and building up the church.[51]

Regarding the matter of deaconesses being ordained in the early Seventh-day Adventist church, it is interesting to note how that practice ceased. In the Church Officers' Gazette of December 1914, it stated that deacons and elders were to be ordained in order to be properly qualified to fulfill their office, but nothing was said about deaconesses' ordination. In the first Adventist Church Manual of 1932, the New Testament origin of deaconess was noted, followed by this statement (which continued to appear in succeeding Church Manuals through 1986), "there is no record, however, that these women were ordained, hence the practice of ordaining deaconesses is not followed by our denomination."[52] It was in the 1990 Church Manual that it was rendered that deaconesses were to participate in an induction service rather than an ordination service.[53] The 2005 Church Manual reveals that this practice continued until the recently held 59th General Conference Session in Atlanta, Georgia on June 24-July 3, 2010. The 2005 manual states, "The church may arrange for a suitable service of induction for the deaconess by an ordained minister holding current credentials."[54] However, the delegates at the 59th General

---

[51]*Ellen G. White Writings*, s.v. "deaconesses," CD-ROM.

[52]Vyhmeister, "Deaconesses in the Church," 23.

[53]Ibid., 24.

[54]General Conference of Seventh-day Adventists, *Church Manual* (Hagerstown: Review and Herald Publishing Assn., 2005), 58.

Conference Session voted that deaconesses should be ordained along with deacons.[55]

Although Ellen White had very little to say about the duties of deaconesses, she forcefully expressed her view that they should be the ones to minister to the female congregants and not the elders. In a letter written to A. T. Jones in September 1902, she scolded him for "listening to the private woes of women—'When a woman comes to you with her troubles, tell her plainly to go to her sisters, to tell her troubles to the deaconesses of the church.'"[56]

Here is some additional information about the duties of deacons and deaconesses in the early Seventh-day Adventist church.

As early as 1856, Joseph Frisbie wrote about deaconesses as church workers. He referred to the choosing of the seven deacons of Acts 6 and Phoebe the deaconess (Rom. 16:1), noting that they "were considered servants, helpers or laborers with the apostles in the gospel, not that they preached the word, but ministered or served their temporal wants." He approvingly quoted from Clarke's commentary: "'There were deaconesses in the primitive church, whose business it was to attend to the female converts at baptism; to instruct the catechumens, or persons who were candidates for baptism: to visit the sick, and those who were in prison; and, in short, perform those religious offices, for the female part of the church, which could not with propriety be performed by men.'"

Frisbie then asked, "Would it not be well then brethren to appoint in all the churches deacons and deaconesses who may answer the qualifications that are laid down clearly in the Bible, with an understanding of what their duties are"? He then summarized these duties:

---

[55]Adventist Review, "Sixth Business Meeting: Proceedings (Church Manual Only)," www.adventistreview.org/article.php?id=3510 (accessed July 5, 2010).

[56]Vyhmeister, "Deaconesses in the Church," 22.

1. To see to the poor and destitute, the widows and orphans, the sick and afflicted
2. To raise funds and care for church finances
3. To make preparation for the ordinances, including keeping on hand good [unfermented] wine from grapes or raisins[57]

Vyhmeister also indicates that J. H. Waggoner published his ideas about "The Office of Deacon" in 1870, emphasizing their spiritual characteristics, based on Acts 6:3 and 1 Tim 3:8-12.[58]

These statements reveal that the duties and responsibilities performed by the deacons and deaconesses of the early Seventh-day Adventist church were in harmony with those carried out by their counterparts in the first century Christian church. They were ordained to provide for the temporal needs of the poor and needy, care for the sick, assist in collecting and managing the funds of the church, teach the Word of God, and make preparations for the ordinances of the church.

---

[57]Ibid.

[58]Ibid.

CHAPTER 5

The Systemic Cause of the Under-Utilization of Deacons and Deaconesses in the Seventh-day Adventist Church

It has been my privilege to conduct training seminars for deacons and deaconesses throughout North America for over a decade. The question that has haunted me for all of these years is why is there so little motivation among the deacons and deaconesses of the Seventh-day Adventist church to reshape their ministry so that it will reflect the ministry of the deacons of the first century Christian church. God placed the burden on my heart to try and find the answer. Therefore, I chose to do a project dissertation on this subject for my doctoral studies.

The project was conducted over a four year period in a church that I was pastoring. At the beginning of the project, the perception that the deacons and deaconesses had of themselves was that they were only to care for the church facilities, collect the offerings, and assist at baptisms and Holy Communion services. This perception was also held by the members. The intervention used in this project challenged this perception but was not able to change it. The most important part of the project for me was to discover that if I presented the deacons and deaconesses with the biblical model for their ministry, provided the training, the tools, the support, and the empowerment; would they have a desire to change the status-quo. My conclusion was that it was difficult for the majority of them to see the need for change. These officers, along with other deacons and deaconesses of the Seventh-day Adventist church, have been adversely affected by several factors.

According to the findings presented in chapter 4, of all of the volumes of books and letters written by Ellen G. White on various topics, the word deacon(s) appears fifteen times. Of those fifteen times, only four relate to their ministry in the early Seventh-day Adventist church. One occurrence deals with a brief discussion on the kind of wine that they were to use in the ordinance of Holy

Communion; two occurrences deal with their responsibility in handling the tithe; and the final occurrence deals with their ordination.[59] The word deaconess(s) appears eighteen times; and only three relate to their ministry in the early Seventh-day Adventist church. Two occurrences reveal that they were ordained along with the deacons and elders; and one occurrence deals with some of their duties—visit the sick, look after the young, and minister to the necessities of the poor.[60]

It is clear that Ellen G. White had very little to say about the duties of the deacons and deaconesses in the early Seventh-day Adventist church. Yet, based upon what she did say and what other early pioneers like Joseph Frisbie and J. H. Waggoner wrote, it appears that the church started out in the 1860s following the model established during the first century Christian church. However, eventually the deacons and deaconesses became less and less responsible for carrying out many of the spiritual duties associated with their office.

In an honest attempt to engage the entire membership of the Seventh-day Adventist church in active ministry, the church created departments such as Personal Ministries and Dorcas/Adventist Community Services. By doing this, some of the most active members—deacons and deaconesses—were rendered almost inactive. The broader ministries that these officers once did were relegated to these departments very early in the history of the Seventh-day Adventist church. The following quotations taken from the church's official website indicate when these departments were introduced.

> Personal Ministries is a facet of the church whose origin can be traced to the beginning of the Seventh-day Adventist history in the 1860s. It endeavors to inspire, motivate, equip, train, and mobilize all members for dynamic Christian service with the conviction that "The church of Christ is organized for service" (Ministry of Healing, p. 148) and "Every son and daughter of God is called to be a missionary; we are called to

---

[59] *Ellen G. White Writings*, s.v. "deacons."

[60] Ibid., s.v. "deaconesses."

the service of God and our fellow men" (*The Ministry of Healing*, p. 395).[61]

In regards to Dorcas/Adventist Community Services, it states:

> Historically, at the General Conference level, Dorcas (later ACS) has been under the Home Missionary, Lay Activities, and Personal Ministries Departments. This ministry of unselfish service started in 1879. Traditionally, Dorcas societies have focused on providing food and clothes to needy people, and remains a part of Adventist Community Services. . . . ACS has expanded its sphere to include many other different types of services and ministries, such as tutoring, job finding and training, community health, elder care, family life and counseling, AIDS programs, etc.[62]

The Personal Ministries Department, Dorcas/Adventist Community Services Department, and all of the other departments of the church are to be commended for the outstanding work that they have done since being established. I am not advocating that they should be abolished. I am simply pointing out that the creation of these departments has caused the church to under-utilize the office of deacon and deaconess, and has caused these officers to lose their identity as spiritual leaders that were originally called to carry out most of the responsibilities that these departments are doing.

To further undermine the spiritual calling of the deaconesses, the church discontinued their ordination for almost a century. And to add insult to injury, proponents for the ordination of female elders and female pastors are misusing Ellen G. White's statement, made in 1895 in favor of the ordination of deaconesses, to support their position. Although the statement was presented in chapter 4, I will repeat it here for the sake of clarity.

---

[61]General Conference of Seventh-day Adventists, "Personal Ministries," http/:www.sabbathschoolpersonalministries.org/article.php?id=3 (accessed May 17, 2009).

[62]General Conference of Seventh-day Adventists, "History of ACSI," http:/www.sabbathschoolpersonalministries.org/article.php?id=49 (accessed May 17, 2009).

Women who are willing to consecrate some of their time to the service of the Lord should be appointed to visit the sick, look after the young, and minister to the necessities of the poor. They should be set apart to this work by prayer and laying on of hands. In some cases they will need to counsel with the church officers or the ministers; but if they are devoted women, maintaining a vital connection with God, they will be a power for good in the church. This is another means of strengthening and building up the church.[63]

The following statement is an example of the misuse of Ellen G. White's counsel to ordain women. Samuel Koranteng-Pipim refutes this misuse. He says,

On the basis of this statement, one writer in Women in Ministry laments: "If only Ellen White's 1895 landmark statement had come fourteen years sooner [in 1881]!" He apparently believes that this "landmark statement" would have encouraged the General Conference committee brethren who were wondering about the question of "perfect propriety" in implementing the alleged 1881 vote to ordain women "who were serving in the gospel ministry." But evidence that Ellen G. White's 1895 statement is not applicable to the ordination of women *as pastors or elders* may be found within the passage itself.[64]

Pipim is correct in his observation that Ellen G. White was not talking about the ordination of women as pastors or elders. However, I will refer to the Ellen G. White Estate to explain who these women were that Ellen G. White was talking about.

There is no documentary evidence that EGW was calling for the ordination of women to gospel ministry in this RH article. The article seems to deal primarily with the question of the

---

[63]*Ellen G. White Writings*, s.v. "deaconesses."

[64]Samuel Koranteng-Pipim, *Must We Be Silent?* (Ann Arbor, MI: Berean Books, 2001), 261.

church utilizing its resources (including women) to the ultimate. The immediate internal context ("visit the sick, look after the young, and minister to the necessities of the poor") may suggest she had in mind the work of a deaconess. The opinion of EGW's personal secretary, Clarence C. Crisler, writing within one year of Mrs. White's death, was to the effect that EGW was referring to ordination of deaconesses rather than gospel ministers.[65]

The discussion of the ordination of female elders and female pastors is beyond the scope of this book. My only intent for mentioning it is to show how this issue has impacted the deaconesses. There is clear evidence from Ellen G. White in favor of the ordination of deaconesses, yet their ordination was discontinued. However, the evidence from Ellen G. White in favor of the ordination of female elders and female pastors is not clear, and the evidence that supports the deaconesses is being misused in an attempt to support female elders and female pastors.

I conclude that because of these underlying factors (1) very little was recorded about the work of deacons and deaconesses during the early history of the Seventh-day Adventist church, (2) other departments were established that eventually supplanted the role and function of deacons and deaconesses, (3) deacons and deaconesses have been marginalized and relegated to caring for the church facilities, collecting tithes and offerings, and serving during Holy Communion and baptism, and (4) the church discontinued the ordination of deaconesses for almost a century but is in continual discussion about the ordination of female elders and female pastors— the church has been sending a negative message over the years to these officers concerning their value and identity as spiritual leaders. Though unintentionally, they have been devalued and displaced. Therefore, the deacons and deaconesses of the Seventh-day Adventist church have been adversely affected subconsciously, and find it very difficult to become motivated to embrace changing the status-quo. Their lack of motivation is systemic. It is due to the tradition and culture of the Seventh-day Adventist church toward the role of these officers from its early history.

---

[65]*Ellen G. White Writings*, s.v. "deaconesses."

CHAPTER 6

Recommendations for Changing the Status-Quo

Margaret Wheatley emphasizes the importance of challenging the status-quo in her quantum theory. To illustrate the importance of change, she points to the adaptability of a stream of water to reconfigure, shift, and create new structures in order to meet the needs of the water's flow. This, she reminds us, is in contrast to the rigid systems of organizations that work against themselves and obstruct their mission for the sake of maintaining the status-quo.[66]

This is an adequate description of the deacons and deaconesses. Due to the systemic problem caused by the tradition and culture of the Seventh-day Adventist church, these officers have held onto a rigid system that has disenfranchised them from the mainstream ministry of the church. The Seventh-day Adventist church needs to adopt a "new structure" that would better meet the needs of the church. I refer to it as a "new structure," but it is not new because it is the structure that was established by the first century Christian church. My use of the phrase a "new structure" is in the same context as Jesus' use of the phrase a "new commandment" in John 13:34. Jesus told His disciples, "A new commandment I give unto you, That ye love one another; as I have loved you, that ye also love one another." The *SDA Bible Commentary* gives this explanation: "The command to love was not in itself new. It belonged to the instructions given by the Lord through Moses (Lev. 19:18). The command was new in that a new demonstration had been given of love, which the disciples were now bidden to emulate."[67] Therefore, in light of this explanation, to adopt a ministry for the deacons and deaconesses of the Seventh-day

---

[66]Margaret J. Wheatley, *Leadership and the New Science: Discovering Order in a Chaotic World*, 2nd ed. (San Francisco: Berrett-Koehler Publishers, 1999), 17-18.

[67]"New Commandment," *SDA Bible Commentary*, 5:1031-1032.

Adventist church that will reflect the ministry of the deacons and deaconesses in the first century Christian church is "new."

The challenge to adopt this new structure without dismantling the current structure and creating a spirit of rivalry is a delicate issue. However, it can be accomplished. In order to accomplish it, I recommend that the local churches become intentional in their efforts to restore the deacons and deaconesses to their biblical position as spiritual leaders of the church. This means that both church officers and members must change their perception of them. When they elect people to serve as deacons and deaconesses, they must elect those who meet the biblical qualifications so that they will have the spiritual gifts and commitment to fulfill the responsibilities required of that office. Rather than limiting them to collecting tithes and offerings, serving during Holy Communion and baptisms, and cleaning the church, utilize their leadership skills by electing each deacon and deaconess, as is possible, to serve as the leader of at least one other department in the church, such as: Personal Ministries leader, Community Services director, Dorcas Society leader, Women's Ministries leader, Sabbath School superintendent/teacher, Stewardship leader, Bible School coordinator, Ministry to People With Disabilities coordinator, Interest coordinator, etc. Those deacons and deaconesses that may not be elected to lead other departments should be encouraged to assist. Just as the elders are customarily assigned to departments as liaisons for the pastor, deacons and deaconesses should also be utilized the same way. They should be utilized along with the elders to visit the members, facilitate mid-week prayer meetings, resolve conflicts in the church, and give Bible studies. They should be provided with sufficient resources to care for the sick and needy. They should be empowered to serve as the physical plant managers.

Now that the Seventh-day Adventist church has taken action to ordain deaconesses again, it is imperative that it provides training for them beyond what has been traditionally given. I recommend to the Seventh-day Adventist church at large that it restore these officers to their biblically defined roles as spiritual leaders. Invite pastors and elders to attend deacon and deaconess training sessions so that they can better understand the role of these officers and the value that they have to contribute to the work. Place as much emphasis on the development of these officers as is placed on the development of local elders, women, singles, children, and youth. Sponsor retreats and summits for them. Produce a handbook for them such as the *Seventh-day Adventist Elder's Handbook* that is produced for the elders. Produce a quarterly magazine for them such as the *Elder's Digest* that is produced for the elders. Train the deacons and deaconesses of newly organized churches so that the current trends will not continue to be perpetuated. When dignity is restored to the office of deaconess, the tension over the ordination of female elders and pastors will be reduced. Women that are called of God to minister will count it a privilege to serve in the office of deaconess. Rather than "re-inventing the wheel," fix the wheel that has been broken.

I also recommend that further study be done on the broader implications of this systemic problem that is the result of the church's hierarchal structure. My deep conviction is that if the Seventh-day Adventist church at large would be willing to dialogue concerning the role and function of deacon and deaconess, beginning at the point of acknowledging that in its zeal to engage the entire church body into active ministry, it crippled one of its members—deacons and deaconesses—and consider implementing the recommendations and principles set forth in this book, the deacons and deaconesses would be restored to their rightful place. They would do ministry in the twenty-first century reflective of the ministry that was done by the deacons and deaconesses of the first century Christian church. The outcome of making such a shift would be as it was of old—"And the word of God increased; and the number of the disciples multiplied in Jerusalem greatly; and a great company of the priests were obedient to the faith" (Acts 6:7). Ellen G. White stated that "this ingathering of souls was due both to the greater freedom secured by the apostles and the zeal and power shown by the seven deacons."[68] And finally, she said, "It is necessary that the same order and system should be maintained in the church now as in the days of the apostles."[69]

---

[68]Ellen White, *The Acts of the Apostles*, 90.

[69]Ellen White, *The Story of Redemption*, 260.

Conclusion

The theology of ministry for deacons and deaconesses is derived from the servant model that was demonstrated in the life of Jesus. Jesus came into the world to minister and not to be ministered unto (Matt 20:28). The act of ministering or serving is inherent in the name deacon and deaconess, and defines the nature of the office.

The deacons that served the first century Christian church solved problems that arose in the church, took care of the needs of the poor, and taught the Word of God. They were ordained to carry out their responsibilities.

The deaconesses that served the first century Christian church took care of the poor and sick among the females, taught the Word of God, assisted women at baptisms, greeted the women entering the church, and directed them to their seats. During the first five centuries, deaconesses were also ordained to carry out their responsibilities.

The deacons that served the early Seventh-day Adventist church provided unfermented grape juice for Holy Communion, collected the tithe, and served as treasurer in the small churches. They were ordained just as their first century counterparts.

The deaconesses that served the early Seventh-day Adventist church visited the sick, looked after the young, ministered to the necessities of the poor, and listened to the women who had troubles that they wanted to share. They were ordained to carry out their responsibilities. However, beginning in 1914 they were no longer ordained. In 1990 the ordination service for deaconesses was replaced with an induction service. However, in June 2010, at the 59th General Conference Session the delegates voted that deaconesses should be ordained along with deacons.

Several underlying factors, which are based upon the tradition and culture of the Seventh-day Adventist church, have created a systemic problem for its deacons and deaconesses. Therefore, these officers are under-utilized and find it difficult to follow the biblical model for their ministry. However, by becoming aware of the problem and being willing to embrace the recommendations for change, the cycle can be broken. Part II will review some of the literature concerning the role of these important church officers.

PART II

The Ministry of Deacons and Deaconesses from the First to the Twenty-First Century

Introduction

Part II consists of a review of the literature relating to the ministry of deacons and deaconesses that will assist the reader of this book to have a better understanding of some of the roles that deacons and deaconesses have served in from the first century to the twenty-first century. It will provide additional information on the debate about whether or not women served as deacons or deaconesses in the first century Christian church. The works cited in Part II are not intended to be exhaustive. However, they represent the most contemporary scholarship in this field.

The next five chapters will put contemporary scholars into conversation with each other. Therefore, you are invited to listen in on their discussions and evaluate their conclusions.

Therefore, brethren, pick out from among you seven men of good repute, full of the Spirit and of wisdom, whom we may appoint to this duty. But we will devote ourselves to prayer and to the ministry of the word. And the word of God increased, and the number of the disciples multiplied in Jerusalem greatly.

Acts 6:3-4, 7 (RSV)

I commend to you our sister Phoebe, a deaconess of the church at Cenchreae, that you may receive her in whatever she may require from you, for she has been a helper of many and of myself as well.

Rom 16:1-2 (RSV)

CHAPTER 7

Women Serving as Deacons
or Deaconesses

Phoebe is the name most referred to by those who propose that female deacons or deaconesses existed in the first century Christian church. Vyhmeister asserts that by the use of the word διάκονος, in Rom 16:1-2, Paul recognized Phoebe as a minister of the church at Cenchrea. She indicates that the word can be translated in various ways, such as: servant, deacon, deaconess, and minister. She states that the way that one chooses to translate it in Rom 16:1-2 "has more to do with the translator than the meaning of the Greek word."[1] Based upon her research, Vyhmeister concludes that Phoebe was a deaconess. She cites the views of some of the early church writers, such as: Origen, John Chrysostom, and Theodoret, to support her view.

Ronald W. Pierce, Rebecca Merrill Groothuis, and Gordon D. Fee arrive at the same conclusion as Vyhmeister; that Phoebe was a deaconess. They suggest that to translate the word διάκονος as servant "would miss the official character of Paul's commendation,"[2] and lessen Phoebe's chances of being welcomed by the church at Rome. They state that "Phoebe was Paul's designated letter carrier to the Roman church. A church's welcome was based on the presentation of credentials. Since Phoebe was a virtual unknown, strong credentials would have been critical in her case. "Servant" would hardly have sufficed in the imperial capital. 'A deacon of the church in Cenchrea' is what was needed."[3]

---

[1]Vyhmeister, "The Ministry of the Deaconess," 17.

[2]Ronald W. Pierce and Rebecca Merrill Grothuis, gen. eds. *Discovering Biblical Equality: Complementarity without Hierarchy*, 2nd ed. Contr. ed. Gordon D. Fee (Downers Grove, IL: InterVarsity Press, 2005), 121.

[3]Ibid.

Like Vyhmeister, Pierce, Groothuis, and Fee, Clarence DeWitt Agan III also agrees that διάκονος can be translated in various ways. His observation is similar to the one that Vyhmeister makes concerning the translation of the word having more to do with the translator than the meaning. Agan says, "It is not difficult to see that one's views of gender, authority, and church office are likely to complicate discussions of this text [Rom 16:1]."[4]

Agan submits that in an attempt to interpret the word διάκονος, in Rom 16:1, many have developed their arguments around two poles: "'Phoebe must be a deacon (or a minister), because she clearly isn't a mere servant;' or, 'Phoebe must be a servant, because she clearly isn't a deacon (or a minister).'"[5] However, based upon lexical evidence, Agan argues that there are more possibilities to consider. The possibilities that he offers are waiter, servant, messenger, and agent. He summarizes his position by saying,

> When Paul refers to Phoebe as a διάκονος, he could be employing the term in any of four senses:
>
> 1. Table Attendance: possibly in reference to a special role played by Phoebe in caring for those facing poverty, and therefore hungry; or if metaphorical, in reference to the humble status associated with "waiters."
> 2. Domestic Attendance: possibly in reference to Phoebe's work in attending to the needs of the church or its members; or, if metaphorical, in reference to the humble status associated with "servants."
> 3. Communication/Delivery: possibly in reference to Phoebe's functioning as a spokesperson, messenger, or representative on behalf of the church.
> 4. Agency/Instrumentality: possibly in reference to Phoebe as an "agent" who carried out the will of or acted in the name of the church (or its elder), in which case Paul

---

[4]Clarence DeWitt "Jimmy" Agan, III, "Deaconesses, and Denominational Discussions: Romans 16:1 as a Test Case," *Presbyterion* 34, no. 2 (Fall 2008): 95.

[5]Ibid., 96.

would most likely intend that she held the office of deacon.[6]

Agan indicates that the use of διάκονος in Rom 16:1 and its immediate context, does not suggest that Paul was using the language of table or domestic attendance, nor of church office. His conclusion is that Phoebe was neither a servant nor a deacon of the church at Cenchrea. She was an emissary, envoy, spokesperson, or possibly, "a traveling representative of her home church when she journeys to Rome."[7]

Therefore, on one hand Agan agrees with Pierce, Groothuis, and Fee, who state that Phoebe was Paul's designated letter carrier. However, he disagrees with their position, as well as Vyhmeister's, that Rom 16:1-2 proves that Phoebe was a female deacon or deaconess. He is careful to add, as he concludes his argument, that he does not disagree that women did (or could) serve as deacons, even if Paul's reference to Phoebe as a διάκονος does not prove it.

Wijngaards proposes that women served as deacons or deaconesses in the first century Christian church. However, he also concludes that the word διάκονος, in Rom 16:1, does not provide this evidence. He states that "the word diakonos applied to Phoebe, does not really carry with it the sense of a precise ministerial function which it will have later where women are concerned. It has here the general sense of 'servant,' which is normal in the New Testament."[8] Wijingaards presents 1 Tim 3:8-12 as evidence that female deacons or deaconesses existed in the first century Christian church. Quoting Jean Daniélou, he states, "'The word "deacon" is here used in its technical sense. It also seems clear that by "the women" in question, who are clearly distinguished from the wives of the deacons while the description of them is parallel to that of the deacons, we must under-

---

[6]Ibid., 105.

[7]Ibid., 106.

[8]John Wijngaards, "The History of Women Deacons," page 1 of 4, http://www.womenpriests.org/tradition/deac_his.asp (accessed October 13, 2008).

stand deaconesses.'"[9] Vyhmeister is in agreement with Wijingaards on this point. She explains that the Greek word for "women" or "wives" has been translated in various ways, such as: "women," with "women deacons" or "their [deacon's] wives" in the note (NRSV); "women," with "either deacons' wives or deaconesses" in the note (NASB); "their wives," with "or deaconesses" in the note (NIV); or "their wives," with their in italics, admitting its absence in the original text (KJV).[10]

Interpreting this text to refer to deacons' wives, conflicts with the fact that the Greek word for wives is not in the possessive. Therefore, Vyhmeister states, "it would not be possible to know whose wives the text was referring to. On the other hand, if one takes the context seriously, these are women who serve the church as do their male counterparts. Quite probably, these women were female deacons."[11] Kevin Madigan and Carolyn Osiek make this observation:

> Two factors suggest that female deacons are referred to here. First is the mention of the female deacon Phoebe at an earlier stage of the development of ministerial structures in the Pauline churches (Rom 16:1-2). Second, the structures of verse 8 about men and verse 11 about women are parallel: the first three words of the Greek text are exactly the same except for gender changes. If female deacons were still referred to by the masculine designation as in Rom 16:1, there would be no other way to make a gender distinction in verse 11, the generic term diakonoi already having been used in verse 8.[12]

---

[9]Ibid., 3.

[10]Nancy Vyhmeister, "Deaconesses in History and in the Seventh-day Adventist Church," *Andrews University Seminary Studies*, vol. 43, no. 1 (2005): 136.

[11]Ibid.

[12]Kevin Madigan and Carolyn Osiek, eds. and trans., *Ordained Women in the Early Church: A Documentary History* (Baltimore, MD: The John Hopkins University Press, 2005), 18.

Deweese supports the previous writers. He quotes this statement that was printed in *The Baptist Magazine* in 1841. It was originally printed with the intent of renewing the emphasis on the work of deaconesses in the Baptist church when their work was on the decline.

> Of the existence of this class of officers in the apostle's time there can be little doubt. We believe that Phoebe was a deaconess, and Euodia and Syntyche, with others; and there is reason to suppose that to such ones the apostle referred when, in 1 Timothy iii.11, he spake of women who were to 'be grave, not slanderers, sober, and faithful in all things.' That he is not there speaking of the wives of deacons, is maintained by very competent authorities, with whom we are inclined to agree.[13]

Gary Straub and James Trader, II concur with the idea that Phoebe carried out the role of a deacon and 1 Tim 3 includes women in the body of deacons.[14] John Franklin Burnett also agrees. He states, "That women were chosen to this sacred office is too well established by the Scriptures [1 Tim 3:8-13] and Church history to be questioned . . . . Phoebe and Priscilla were deaconesses, and fellow-servants with Paul."[15]

Ute E. Eisen presents some interesting discoveries from the inscriptions written on the tombstones of female deacons or deaconesses during the fourth through the seventh centuries. In this statement, he predates proof of their existence in Asia Minor to the second century.

> The number of surviving inscriptions concerning women deacons in Asia Minor is very extensive. Very early, 1 Tim

---

[13]Charles W. Deweese, *Women Deacons and Deaconesses: 400 Years of Baptist Service* (Macon, GA: Mercer University Press, 2005), 67.

[14]Gary Straub and James Trader, II, *Your Calling as a Deacon* (St. Louis, MO: Chalice Press, 2005), 17, 22.

[15]John Franklin Burnett, *The Church the Pillar and Ground of the Truth* (1917; repr., Charleston, SC: BiblioLife, 2009), 65.

3:11 and Pliny, Ep. X, 96, 8 attest the presence of women
deacons in Asia Minor in the second century. The abundant
epigraphic evidence suggests the continuity of an office of
women deacons in Asia Minor from the very beginning.[16]

Based upon inscriptions written on the tombstones of the husbands of
female deacons or deaconesses, it can be concluded that them holding
the office of deacon was not dependent upon their husbands being
deacons. A woman deacon named Basilissa dedicated an inscription to
her deceased husband and his family. The inscription reads: "The first
man of the village, Quintus, son of Heraclius, with his wife Matrona
and his children Anicetus and Catilla, all four lie in this grave. The
wife of Anicetus, the deacon Basilissa, has erected this pleasant tomb
together with her only son Numitorius, who is still an immature
child."[17] Three things can be deducted from this inscription. The first
thing is that "it is certain that Basilissa was an officeholder in the
church, while her husband bears no official title."[18] Therefore, the
church during the second century did not require women to be
married to male deacons in order to serve as female deacons, as some
interpret 1 Tim 3:11. A better interpretation is that these women are
women deacons whether they were married to male deacons or not.
Another example of this is the "deacon Strategis from Goslu, who
together with her son Pankratios dedicated a gravestone to her
husband Menneas, her sister-in-law Alexandria, and her son
Domnos."[19]

The second deduction is that women deacons were not in every
case required to be virgins. It varied according to regions. Here are
two examples of women deacons in Macedonia, the region of Edessa.
One of them is a virgin, the other is not. The inscriptions read
"Monument of Agathokleia, the virgin and deacon." "Monument of

---

[16]Ute E. Eisen, *Women Officeholders in Early Christianity: Epigraphical and Literary* (Collegeville, MN: The Liturgical Press, 2000), 173-174.

[17]Ibid., 168.

[18]Ibid.

[19]Ibid.

the deacon Theodosia and the virgins Aspelia (Aspilia ?) and Agathokleia."[20] Therefore, virgins and women deacons were two distinct groups. The family situation of these women in Asia Minor varied. Many of them were wives and mothers, and others were members of monastic orders. However, the family situation of women deacons in the region of Moab was different.

> None of the women named in the inscriptions is connected with a family of her own [same as] for the male deacons of this region. This points to the probability that the epigraphically attested women deacons of this time and region lived celibate lives, as demanded by Canon 15 of the Council of Chalcedon [451] for all officeholders with the exception of lectors and cantors.[21]

The third and final deduction is that the women deacons and widows were two distinct groups. Wijngaards agrees with this assessment. "During the first centuries, however, confusion in terminology and practice remained. In 517 AD the Synod of Epaon speaks of 'widows whom they call deaconesses.' Deaconesses are sometimes referred to as 'widow and deaconess.' It is likely, however, that the two roles have always been somewhat distinct."[22]

Four widows above sixty years of age were elected to serve the Broadmead Baptist Church in Bristol, England in 1679 based upon them agreeing that they would not remarry, according to 1 Tim 5:11.[23] In light of this, Deweese explains that it is not the primary view of Baptists that the origin of women deacons resides with the widows of 1 Tim 5. However, he states that some Baptists do relate these two

---

[20]Ibid., 181.

[21]Ibid., 162.

[22]Wijngaards, 3.

[23]Deweese, *Women Deacons and Deaconesses: 400 Years of Baptist Service*, 54.

groups. E. Glenn Hinson states that it appears that the New Testament women deacons were selected from the widows.[24]

Another discovery that Eisen makes is that all of these women officeholders held the official title of διάκονος or διακόνισσα (deacon or deaconess). On some of their tombstone inscriptions, the title was abbreviated as διακ or δκ. Also, the inscription on the tombstone of a deacon Maria states that she died at the age of thirty-eight. This indicates that young women were ordained to the diaconate during the seventh century.[25]

---

[24]Ibid., 39.

[25]Eisen, 161.

CHAPTER 8

Deacons and Deaconesses
as Teachers of God's Word

There are few authors who have written recently about the role of deacons and deaconesses as teachers of God's Word. The reason for the lack of literature could be because little is recorded in the New Testament concerning it. Stephen and Philip are mentioned as examples of deacons serving in this role (Acts 6:8-60, 8:5-40). However, Owen Chadwick says, "Stephen and Philip were deacons who preached but they were exceptions."[26] Although he does not elaborate, Richard R. Gaillardetz acknowledges that the ministry of preaching and the ministry of catechesis were among the broad range of ministries performed by deacons throughout church history.[27] John M. Huels confirms, according to the *Didascalia Apostolorum* (early third century), one of the important roles of deaconesses was in the catechesis.[28] Vyhmeister elaborates more on this point by stating exactly what the *Didascalia* says about the teaching role of deaconesses. She quotes, "And when she who is being baptized has come up from the water, let the deaconess receive her, and teach and educate her in order that the unbreakable seal of baptism shall be (kept) in chastity and holiness. On this account, we say that the ministry of a woman deacon is especially required and urgent."[29]

---

[26]Owen Chadwick, *The Early Reformation on the Continent* (New York: Oxford University Press, 2001), 104.

[27]Richard R. Gaillardetz, *The Church in the Making: Lumen Gentium, Christus Dominus, Orientalium Ecclesiarum* (Mahwah, NJ: Paulist Press, 2006), 184.

[28]John M. Huels, "Special Questions on the Diaconate," *Liturgical Ministry* 13 (Winter 2004): 1.

[29]Vyhmeister, "Deaconesses in History and in the Seventh-day Adventist Church," 141.

One of the roles of the Baptist deaconesses in 1679 was to "speak a word to their souls [the sick], as occasion requires, for support or consolation, to build them up in a spiritual lively faith in Jesus Christ."[30] This indicates that deaconesses were to teach God's Word.

Alice Morse Earle says also during the 1600s that deacons "dispensed the word on Sabbaths to the congregation during the absence of the ordained minister."[31]

Benjamin L. Merkle, however, disagrees with the idea that deacons and deaconesses are to serve as teachers of God's Word. He says, "Deacons are called to 'hold' to the faith with a clear conscience, but they are not called to 'teach' that faith (1 Tim. 3:9). This suggests that the deacons do not have an official teaching role in the church."[32] To further strengthen his position, Merkle quotes D.A. Carson who states, "'Deacons were responsible to serve the church in a variety of subsidiary roles, but enjoyed no church-recognized teaching authority akin to that of elders.'"[33] However, Merkle concludes that although deacons are not required to teach, does not mean they are not permitted to teach. They should teach God's Word when situations demand it.

Rosalind Brown, although an Anglican, writes from a wider Christian tradition. She states that proclaiming the gospel is one of three strands that makes up the diaconal ministry.[34] Even though preaching during the main worship service is not necessarily the role of deacons, Brown says that it is appropriate that they be trained to preach. This training prepares them to present God's Word within the varying context of their ministry. Brown gives the following examples

---

[30]Deweese, *Women Deacons and Deaconesses: 400 Years of Baptist Service*, 54.

[31]Alice Morse Earle, *Sabbath in Puritan New England*, 7th ed. (Teddington, Middlesex: The Echo Library, 2007), 57.

[32]Benjamin L. Merkle, *40 Questions about Elders and Deacons* (Grand Rapids: Kregel Publications, 2008), 238.

[33]Ibid.

[34]Rosalind Brown, *Being a Deacon Today* (Harrisburg, PA: Morehouse Publishing, 2005), xi.

to show the importance of deacons being trained to preach/proclaim the gospel: (1) a deacon may be requested to preach at a baptism, wedding, or funeral, especially when he or she has been the catalyst for the person coming to church; (2) if a deacon is also active in the local school during the week he or she can help connect people to the church; (3) conducting services during nursing home visits; (4) leading a small Bible study group or an inquirers' group; (5) sitting in someone's living room discussing a favorite Bible text with them; or (6) conducting a bedside communion during a hospital visit.[35]

According to Brown, deacons are charged to reflect on Scripture with God's people so that the whole church is equipped to live out the gospel in the world. When a deacon fails to do this, Brown says,

> The deacon's own ministry in the world will suffer because he or she will be doing it all on behalf of people who see no need to be engaged for themselves. However, if the deacon who is known to be actively engaged in ministry in the world is the same person who reflects with the people of God on God's word and their own vocation to serve God, who catechizes and leads them by example in living the gospel wherever they are, then there can be no excuse for anyone to drive a wedge between seeking nourishment in Scripture and getting deeply involved in the world: there is no option of it being 'either/or' since the deacon embodies the complementarity.[36]

Sebastian S. Karambai, a Roman Catholic,[37] and the bishops of the Church of England,[38] agree with the previous mentioned writers

---

[35]Ibid., 80-82.

[36]Ibid., 82.

[37]Sebastian S. Karambai, *Ministers and Ministries in the Local Church: A Comprehensive Guide to Ecclesiastical Norms* (Bandra, Mumbai: The Bombay Saint Paul Society, 2005), 182.

[38]Church of England, *For Such a Time as This: A Renewed Diaconate in the Church of England* (London: Church House Publishing, 2001), 51.

that one of the primary functions of deacons is to proclaim/preach the Word of God.

CHAPTER 9

Deacons and Deaconesses as Care Givers to the Sick and Needy

Eurico Tadeu Xavier concludes that the work of deacons and deaconesses is indispensable to the Seventh-day Adventist church. Among all of the services that they render, caring for the sick and helping the poor and suffering are important responsibilities that they carry out. He also states that the deacons or deaconesses may accompany an ordained minister or elder of the church to give communion to a homebound member who happened to be sick, or for any other reason could not leave home to participate in the communion service.[39]

The *Seventh-day Adventist Church Manual* includes the care of the sick and the poor in its list of duties for deacons and deaconesses. It records the following:

> Another important responsibility of deacons is the care of the sick, relieving the poor, and aiding the unfortunate. Money should be provided for this work from the church fund for the needy. The treasurer, on recommendation from the church board, will pass over to the deacons or deaconesses whatever may be needed for use in needy cases. This work is the particular charge of the deacons and the deaconesses, but the church is to be kept fully acquainted with the needs, in order to enlist the membership's support.[40]

The bishops of the Church of England are in agreement with Xavier's and the *Church Manual's* views of the ministry of deacons to the poor and sick. They state that "A deacon is called to serve the Church of God, and to work with its members in caring for the poor,

---

[39]Eurico Tadeu Xavier, "Deacons Take Care of Almost Everything," trans. Antonio A. Rios, *Elder's Digest* 10, January-March 2004, 6-7.

[40]General Conference of Seventh-day Adventists, *Church Manual*, 57.

the needy, the sick, and all who are in trouble."[41] They suggest that deacons may team up with ordained and lay ministers of the church to carry out this specialized area of pastoral ministry. This ministry would also include "the lonely and those who are ground down by adverse circumstances or by the pressures of life at home or work."[42] Straub and Trader indicate that one of the responsibilities of the deacons in the Presbyterian church is to see to members who are sick and in need.[43] They also state that after the Protestant Reformation, Protestant churches re-examined the roles of the deacon. Some churches decided that in addition to other duties, deacons work with homebound members.[44] Earl S. Johnson also states that the duty of the Presbyterian deacon is "first of all, to minister to those who are in need, to the sick, to the friendless, and to any who may be in distress both within and beyond the community of faith."[45] Johnson also adds that deacons assist senior citizens and visit shut-ins or members who cannot attend church services regularly. They organize transportation for those who cannot drive to their medical appointments. They provide meals and housing for the homeless, organize advocacy programs for those in legal trouble, and minister to those in jails and prisons.[46] Karambai says that deacons are to support the families under their care in their difficulties, alleviate the suffering of the sick, and be involved in the administration of goods and in the church's charitable activities.[47]

------

[41]Church of England, 51.

[42]Ibid., 54

[43]Straub and Trader, II, 20.

[44]Ibid., 18.

[45]Earl S. Johnson, Jr., *The Presbyterian Deacon: An Essential Guide* (Louisville, KY: Geneva Press, 2002), 28.

[46]Ibid., 31.

[47]Karambai, 183-184.

Gaillardetz says that according to early documentary testimony deacons ministered to the sick.[48] Burnett says that "deacons were God's first ministers to the poor."[49] Chadwick also agrees. He observes that the ministry of the deacons in the New Testament was to give out alms and look after the poor.[50] He states that "Calvin said that deacons were of two kind, those who looked after the poor and those who cared for the sick, and both kinds were to be called deacons."[51]

Of all of the tombstone inscriptions that Eisen presents, only one makes reference to the kind of work that the women deacons did during the second to the seventh centuries. The inscription on the tombstone of a deacon Maria from Cappadocia in Asia Minor, sixth century, indicates that she took care of the needy. It reads, "Here lies the deacon Maria of pious and blessed memory, who according to the words of the apostle raised children, sheltered guests, washed the feet of the saints, and shared her bread with the needy. Remember her, Lord, when she comes into your kingdom."[52]

Vyhmeister cites from the *Apostolic Constitutions* that the deaconesses of the early church "ministered to the sick, the poor, and those in prison."[53] She also relates the description of an ancient deaconess in Holland during the 1500s. She quotes the Puritan governor William Bradford who described the ancient deaconess in his work entitled *Dialogue*.

> 'She did frequently visit the sick and weak, especially women, and, as there was need, called out maids and young women to

---

[48]Gaillardetz, 184.

[49]Burnett, 62.

[50]Chadwick, 104.

[51]Ibid., 105.

[52]Eisen, 164-167.

[53]Vyhmeister, "Deaconesses in History and in the Seventh-day Adventist Church," 141.

watch and do them other help as their necessity did require; and if they were poor, she would gather relief for them of those that were able, or acquaint the deacons; and she was obeyed as a mother in Israel and an officer of Christ.'[54]

Vyhmeister refers to a 1956 article in *Ministry* by Bess Ninaj, which states that "deaconesses should care for the sick and the poor, which 'may involve financial assistance, personal help with children in the home, assistance with household duties, or making arrangements for any or all of these.'"[55]

The earliest detailed list of deaconess duties in Baptist literature was developed in 1679 and presented to four widows above sixty years of age. They were elected to serve as deaconesses of the Broadmead Baptist Church in Bristol, England. These were their responsibilities:

1. To visit the sick, to have their eye and ear open to hearken and inquire who is sick, and to visit the sick sisters; in an especial manner to see what they need, because it may not be so proper for men in several cases.
2. To visit not only sick sisters, but sick brethren also; and therefore some conceive [this] may be the reason why they must be sixty years of age, that none occasion [of offence] may be given; as 1 Tim. v. 14.
3. Not only to take care of their sick bodies, of the brethren and sisters, but that their wants may be supplied; and therefore to make reports back of their condition, to the elders and deacons of the congregation.
4. It is their duty also to speak a word to their souls, as occasion requires, for support or consolation, to build them up in a spiritual lively faith in Jesus Christ. For as some observe, there is not an office of Christ in his church, but it is dipped in the blood of our Lord Jesus.

---

[54]Ibid., 145.

[55]Ibid., 154-155.

> Some think it is their duty to attend the sick; and if so, then they are to be maintained by the church.[56]

These responsibilities show that those deaconesses served as care givers to the sick and needy.

Earle states that during the 1600s deaconesses also visited the sick and afflicted in the community, and the deacons provided for the poor of the church.[57]

Chadwick also points out that during the 1500s, deacons and deaconesses were used as managers of hospitals in the Netherlands.[58] Huels mentions the importance of the deaconesses' role of nursing and pastoral care during the third century.[59]

Janice Rider Ellis and Celia Love Hartley, recounting the history of the nursing profession, states, "The deaconesses of the Eastern Christian Church represent one group of particular significance to the history of nursing. These dedicated young women practiced 'works of mercy' that included feeding the hungry, clothing the naked, visiting the imprisoned, sheltering the homeless, caring for the sick, and burying the dead."[60] Ellis and Hartley state that these deaconesses are often cited as being the earliest counterparts to the community health nurses of today. They carried a basket that contained food and medicine that they distributed as they visited the homes of the sick. Their basket is the forerunner of the contemporary visiting nurse's bag. Phoebe is often referred to as the first deaconess and first visiting nurse in books about nursing history.

The Order of Widows and the Order of Virgins also visited the sick in their homes, and were

---

[56]Deweese, *Women Deacons and Deaconesses: 400 Years of Baptist Service*, 53-54.

[57]Earle, 62, 57.

[58]Chadwick, 105.

[59]Huels, 1.

[60]Janice Rider Ellis and Celia Love Hartley, *Nursing in Today's World: Trends, Issues and Management*, 8th ed. (Philadelphia, PA: Lippincott Williams & Wilkins, 2004), 117.

often mentioned along with the deaconesses as being the earliest organized group of public health nurses. The movement peaked in Constantinople in about 400 A.D., when a staff of 40 deaconesses lived and worked under the direction of Olympia, a powerful and deeply religious deaconess. The influence of the deaconess order diminished in the 5th and 6th centuries, when church decrees removed clerical duties and rank from the deaconess.[61]

Ellis and Hartley continue relating the important role that deaconesses played as forerunners to today's nurses. They state that in Europe, Pastor Theodore Fliedner and his wife Friederike revived the deaconess movement by establishing a training institute for deaconesses at Kaisewerth, Germany in 1836.

Later they [the Fliedners] opened a small hospital for the sick, and Gertrude Reichardt, the daughter of a physician, was recruited as their first deaconess. The endeavors at Kaiserwerth included care of the sick, visitations and parochial work, and teaching. A course in nursing was developed that included lectures by physicians. In 1849, Pastor Fliedner traveled to the United States, where he helped to establish the first motherhouse of Kaiserwerth deaconesses in Pittsburgh, Pennsylvania. With the help of four deaconesses, the Motherhouse of Kaiserwerth Deaconesses assumed responsibility for the Pittsburgh Infirmary, which was the first Protestant hospital in the United States. The hospital is now called Passavant Hospital.[62]

A great legacy has been left by the deaconesses of past generations. If deaconesses of the twenty-first century would continue this legacy of working with the nurses in their churches and communities, they could alleviate a lot of suffering among the sick and needy.

---

[61]Ibid.

[62]Ibid., 123.

CHAPTER 10

Deacons and Deaconesses
as Conflict Managers

Diana Davis takes her readers back to the election of the first deacons that served the first century Christian church. She says that Acts 6:1-7 is a biblical account of a conflict within the early church. Straub and Trader ask, "Did you notice that the office of deacon arose out of a conflict?"[63] Davis says, "There was trouble in the church. There were rumblings that some of the widows weren't receiving a fair portion in the daily distribution of food. Conflict."[64] Davis describes the outcome of electing the seven deacons as a win-win situation. The church was pleased, the complainers were appeased, the widows were cared for, and the apostles' ministry of prayer and preaching was not interrupted. She points out that these seven men were not called to serve the church as a board of directors or administrators. They were called to solve church problems. Davis applies the role that the deacons of the first century Christian church played in managing conflict to deacons of the twenty-first century. She says, "When conflict arises, deacons must act with dignity. As they lovingly 'step up to the plate' to calm adversity and help with the problem, their wives can also assist with peacemaking."[65]

Davis tells the story about her and her husband conducting a national conference for deacons and deacon wives. Her husband gave each deacon two buckets to carry around with them for the entire week. One bucket had a large W written on it, and the other one had a large G. "Steve told those deacons that every deacon carries two buckets: one filled with water and the other filled with gasoline. When a church fire, or problem, arises, it is a deacon's responsibility to pour

---

[63]Staub and Trader, II, 27.

[64]Diana Davis, *Deacon Wives: Fresh Ideas to Encourage Your Husband and the Church* (Nashville: B & H Publishing Group, 2009), 89-90.

[65]Ibid., 90.

water on that problem, not gas! When asked about the buckets, the deacons explained the problem-solving responsibility of deacons in the church."[66]

Anthony B. Robinson and Robert W. Wall also appeal to the account in Acts to show the important role that deacons play in managing conflict in the church. Their analysis of the events of Acts 6 is that Luke, the writer of Acts,

> states the failure of infrastructure as a breakdown in the daily diakonia ('distribution') of food (6:1) and his subsequent use of the verbal form diakoneo ('wait on tables') assesses this conflict: food is not being 'distributed' to the needy. Finally, the repetition of diakonia in verse 4 introduces the resolution of this conflict: the apostles are no longer diverted by administrative tasks and are fully engaged in their diakonia ('ministry') of the Word.[67]

Although Robinson and Wall focus their readers' attention on the conflict managing skills of the apostles who identified the problem and initiated the process, it cannot be denied that those who were elected as deacons were the actual practitioners that brought about resolution.

Penny Edgell Becker interviewed twenty-three church congregations in Oak Park, IL to find out what kind of conflicts they were encountering and how they were dealing with them. One incident that she records is about a conflict that arose in the Bethlehem Congregational Church over the use of gender-exclusive language in the Sunday services. After a discussion in a Sunday school class, a group of well-educated professional women approached the deacons and asked, "What can we do about changing things?"[68] The deacons conducted a series of public meeting to ascertain how the

---

[66]Ibid., 91.

[67]Anthony B. Robinson and Robert W. Wall, *Called to be Church: The Book of Acts for a New Day* (Grand Rapids: Wm. B. Eerdmans Publishing, 2006), 92.

[68]Penny Edgell Becker, *Congregations in Conflict: Cultural Models of Local Religious Life* (New York: Cambridge University Press, 1999), 101.

other members felt about this issue. The pastor attended the meetings but did not chair them. Neither did he voice his position on the issue. Becker states that the pastor explained to her that his role was to ensure that the process of making the decision was caring and open. The process lasted over a year and a half with an agreed upon outcome for change.[69] This is an example of deacons serving in the role of conflict managers.

Adele Oltman writes about events that occurred in the African American community in Savannah, GA beginning sixty years after Abraham Lincoln signed the Emancipation Proclamation. One event that she relates involves the board of deacons resolving a conflict at the First African Church in 1928. The wife of a deacon left the church because she felt that her husband had been mistreated by the pastor. The deacons dealt with this conflict by setting with her "'in prayer and meditation to God,' endeavoring to convince their 'sister to come back and be reconciled with us in our church.'"[70] She declined to stay. However, she returned one year later, after the deacons recommended restoring her husband to the deacon board. She appeared before the deacons to apologize and asked for forgiveness. They and the church forgave her.

Oltman shows that the deacons of the African American churches in Savannah were responsible for recommending that members who violated church laws be disciplined by the church. Depending upon the offence, the discipline could be the hand of Fellowship withdrawn from them and they be excluded from the church, or they be required to make a public acknowledgment and ask the church's forgiveness.[71]

Thomas R. Burns sees the need for deacons to receive training in basic counseling so that they can become effective in this area of their ministry. He says that deacons "may be called upon to provide counseling for family problems arising from domestic violence, financial crises, marriage or family relationship problems, parent/child

---

[69]Ibid., 101-102.

[70]Adele Oltman, *Sacred Mission, Worldly Ambition: Black Christian Nationalism in the Age of Jim Crow* (Athens, GA: University of Georgia Press, 2008), 159.

[71]Ibid., 161.

problems, pre-marital counseling, as well as the need for spiritual advice."[72] Burns introduces a four-step problem-solving method that can be used by deacons as they counsel with individuals and families in conflict. The four steps are: identification of the problem, assessment of alternatives, decision-making among the alternatives, and implementation of an alternative.[73] I also recognize that deacons and deaconesses are called to serve as conflict managers and need to develop counseling skills. Like Burns, I suggest steps for these officers to use when helping individuals to solve problems. I offer a nine step problem-solving process, which includes: engagement, assessment, definition, setting goals, alternatives, contract, action, evaluation, and continuation. In my previous book, I included a case study to show how this process can be implemented by deacons and deaconesses.[74] It is important that these officers have a professional counselor to whom they can refer people with problems too difficult for them to address. I suggest that they develop interdisciplinary teams consisting of church members that work in the helping professions. These individuals can be of great assistance to them. I have included the problem-solving process in chapter 19 of this book.

---

[72]Thomas R. Burns, *Basic Counseling for Deacons: A Guide for Interviewing* (Rio Rancho, NM: Thomas Burns, 2008), 58.

[73]Ibid., 57.

[74]Vincent White, 48-58.

CHAPTER 11

Deacons and Deaconesses as Business Managers

Deweese makes reference to the work of R. B. C. Howell, a Baptist pastor whose writings were very influential to the Baptist church during the 1800s. Deweese says although Howell favored deaconesses, he influenced the Baptist in the 1800s to assign administrative, business, and financial matters to male deacon bodies, thereby excluding women.

> He claimed that deacons 'of right have the full control' over the church's temporalities. They must exercise 'management' over the church's 'property and funds,' although he did make clear that such management 'is not absolute, but limited to such uses as the church may order.' Deacons were both 'the financial officers of the church, and 'a BOARD OF OFFICERS, or the executive board of the church, for her temporal department.'(This designation of a deacon body as a 'board (of managers)' continues to have implications for many Baptist churches in the early 2000s.)[75]

Some historical facts that may have led Howell to this way of thinking can be gathered from Dwight A. Moody's sermon, preached on June 15, 1997. Moody asks two important questions. The first one is why was there a decline in deaconesses during the nineteenth century? The second is, what influence do cultural trends have to do with it? Moody submits that the emergence of the all male corporate board of directors in American society during the second half of the nineteenth century influenced the way in which the church was managed. He says, "Deacons drifted away from ministry and toward management. While churches were once open to women sharing ministry responsibilities, they were closed to the idea of women

---

[75]Deweese, *Women Deacons and Deaconesses: 400 Years of Baptist Service*, 71-72.

sharing in the management decisions."[76] Moody's observation seems to suggest that Howell's views were influenced by the secular management culture of the nineteenth century. He, in turn, influenced the Baptist church to assign the role of business managers to the male deacon board. This was an act of retrogression for deaconesses. They were just beginning to revive in the 1830s, after virtually being discontinued in the middle ages by the Christian church.[77]

Annie Barksdale, in her description of the role of deacons, says that they should also be trained in church management.[78] William Speer also includes in his list of deacons' responsibilities, "the management of the temporal affairs of the Church."[79] James Hastings agrees with this concept. Speaking of deacons and bishops in the early church, he says, "The charities of the church and the maintenance of its ministry (1 Co 9:7-14, Gal 6:5) required business management."[80] He therefore, implies that both of these officers are to be involved in the business management of the church.

Bill Pitts interviewed the key participants in the election of the first women deacons in the First Baptist Church of Waco, Texas in 1996. He cites Alton Pearson, chairman of the deacons at the time of that event, who stated, "'Deacons, are for service, not to run the church.'"[81] According to Pitts, Pearson "resisted the image of a board

---

[76]Dwight A. Moody, *Heaven for a Dime: Memoir of a Small Town Preacher* (Lincoln, NE: Winter's Showcase, 2002), 58.

[77] Nichols, 12-13.

[78]Annie Barksdale, *The Holy Spirit* (Stamford, CT: Annie Barksdale, 2002), 112.

[79]William Speer, *God's Rule for Christian Giving: A Practical Essay on the Source of Christian Economy* (1923; repr., Charleston, SC: BiblioLife, 2009), 158.

[80]James Hastings, ed., *A Dictionary of the Bible*, vol. 3, pt. 2 (Honolulu: University Press of the Pacific, 2004), 727.

[81]Bill Pitts, "Women, Ministry, and Identity: Establishing Female Deacons at First Baptist Church, Waco, Texas," *Baptist History and Heritage* 42, no. 1 (Winter 2007): 76.

of deacons that existed merely to make financial decisions."[82] This statement by Pearson shows that he is opposed to the idea that deacons should serve as business managers of the church. Therefore, he disagrees with Howell's ideology that deacons should serve as the financial officers and executive board of the church.

The *Seventh-day Adventist Church Manual* does not advocate deacons as business managers but physical plant managers. It states:

> It is the deacon's duty to see that the building is kept clean and in repair, and that the grounds upon which the church stands are kept clean and made attractive. This also includes ensuring that the janitorial work is done. In large churches it is often necessary to employ a janitor. The deacons should recommend a suitable person to the church board, which takes action by vote to employ such help, or the church board may authorize the deacons to employ a janitor. Church board authorization should be obtained for all major repair expenses. All bills for repairs, as well as for water, light, fuel, et cetera, are referred to the church treasurer for payment.[83]

Based upon this statement the church board serves as the body that makes the financial decisions and not the board of deacons in the Seventh-day Adventist church.

Conclusion

It may be concluded from the review of the works in chapters 7-11 that the New Testament reveals little information about the existence of female deacons or deaconesses and the role that they played in the first century Christian church. In that the Greek word διάκονος can be translated in various ways, the way in which it is translated to describe Phoebe's position (the woman most referred to as proof that female deacons/deaconesses existed, Rom 16:1-2)

---

[82]Ibid.

[83]General Conference of Seventh-day Adventists, *Church Manual*, 71-72.

depends upon the presupposition of the translator. Similar ambivalence surrounds the interpretation of the Greek word for "wives" in 1 Tim 3:11 KJV, whether it should be translated so that the text means deacons' wives or women deacons/deaconesses. However, in the absence of the possessive form of διάκονος, the context is most favorable to the translation of "women," meaning women deacons/deaconesses.

Clear evidence beginning as early as the third century substantiates that female deacons/deaconesses existed. Some of the evidences are documented in the *Didascalia Apostolorum* (third century), the *Apostolic Constitutions* (late fourth century), inscriptions written on the tombstones of female deacons/deaconesses during the fourth through the seventh centuries, and current literature from both Protestant and Catholic writers. These women deacons were a distinct group from the virgins or the widows of 1 Tim 5. In some cases a woman deacon was a virgin or a widow. But that was not the criteria.

There are four important roles in which deacons and deaconesses function. The first is the role of teachers of God's Word. Although their ministry does not consist of preaching God's Word during the main worship service, they should be able to teach when the occasion requires them to. One of their primary functions is to proclaim the Word of God. Therefore, they should be able to teach a Bible study group, explain a Bible passage during a nursing home, hospital, or home visit, and teach the members how to study the Bible and explain it to others. Deacons and deaconesses that are exceptionally gifted in teaching and/or preaching the Word of God, as were Stephen and Philip, could also conduct evangelistic meetings.

The second role in which deacons and deaconesses are to function is that of serving as care givers to the sick and needy. These officers are to render help to the sick, poor and suffering, troubled, lonely, homebound, friendless, and senior citizens. They are to provide meals and housing for the homeless, organize transportation for those who cannot drive to their medical appointments, organize advocacy programs for those needing legal assistance, provide financial assistance to the poor, help with children in the homes, and assist with household duties. Deacons and deaconesses may team up with ordained and lay ministers of the church to carry out this ministry.

The third role of these officers is the role of conflict managers. The office of deacon in the first century Christian church arose out of a conflict over the daily distribution of food for the widows. These officers were called to solve problems that arose in the church. This is still their role in the twenty-first century. They are to calm adversities and help with the problems in the church so that the pastor and elders are not distracted from preaching, prayer, and meditation. Deacons and deaconesses are to assess disciplinary issues that exist among members and recommend what action the church should take. They may also be called upon to provide counseling for family problems arising from domestic violence, financial crises, marriage or family relationship problems, parent/child problems, pre-marital counseling, or the need for spiritual advice. Therefore, it is important that these officers receive training in basic counseling so that they can become effective in this area of ministry.

The fourth and final role is primarily carried out by a board of all male deacons. It is the role of business managers. Baptist churches began assigning this role to their deacons during the 1800s. They were influenced by the cultural trends of American society to adopt this style of management. During the second half of the nineteenth century, the all male corporate board of directors emerged. As the churches embraced this style of management, deacons drifted away from ministry and focused their attention on management. The exclusion of women deacons or deaconesses in management decisions was a factor in the decline of the deaconesses during the nineteenth century. Some churches still assign the role of business managers to their deacons. Others believe that "'Deacons are for service, not to run the church.'"[84]

There are two questions that I propose as being worthy of future research. The first question is how did the use or misuse of power obtained by deacons to run the church as business managers during the nineteenth century influence the way in which the Seventh-day Adventist church defines the role of its deacons and deaconesses? The second question is, is the under-utilization of the deacons and deaconesses of the Seventh-day Adventist church a reaction to the use or misuse of power obtained by the aforementioned deacons? The results of such research could serve as a catalyst for the Seventh-day Adventist church to readdress the role of deacons and deaconesses, and provide more training for them.

---

[84]Ibid.

The relationship between the literature review and the central topic of this book is to aid in the development of a balanced ministry for the deacons and deaconesses of the Seventh-day Adventist church that will empower them to serve in the role of teachers of God's Word, care givers to the sick and needy, conflict managers, and "physical plant managers" that maintain the upkeep of the church's property. The emphasis is on creating a balance between empowering these officers to utilize all of their God-given gifts in service to the church, and not misuse their power to "run" the church as business managers.

PART III

Implications for Deacon and Deaconess Ministry Based upon First Century and Old Testament Counterparts

Introduction

There are several implications for the ministry of deacons and deaconesses in the twenty-first century that can be drawn from the ministry of the deacons in the first century Christian church. For example, the first century Christian church used the representative form of government in the election of the original seven deacons. This was established by God for His church since the time of Moses. The "multitude of the disciples" that was involved in that election process was spiritually connected with God and led by the Holy Spirit. Therefore, they understood the spiritual qualifications that the candidates needed to possess, and were committed to selecting only those who possessed such qualifications. The implications of this for the church in the twenty-first century are to continue to follow the representative form of government in electing deacons and deaconesses, give serious thought and prayer before putting a person in this office, make sure that those being elected meet the biblical qualifications, and those who feel that they are not ready to assume such awesome responsibilities should decline and request to be placed in a training capacity until they are confident that God is directing them to serve.

A primary task of the deacons of the first century Christian church was conflict resolution. The conflict that faced the church required that these men serve tables and take care of the daily distribution of assistance to the Grecian and Hebrew widows. The deacons also taught and preached the Word of God, and nurtured the church members. The implication of this for the deacons and deaconesses in the twenty-first century is that they assess the physical, social, emotional, and spiritual needs of the church members. Then they should seek ways to meet those needs. This would include but not be limited to: (1) visiting the members; (2) seeing that the church has an equitable system in place for meeting the needs of its needy members; (3) conducting Bible studies; (4) leading out in prayer groups; (5) assisting in and conducting public evangelistic meetings; (6) seeking ways to minister to the community in which the church is located; and (7) discipling new members.

The sons of Korah are the Old Testament counterparts of the New Testament deacons and deaconesses. They were also referred to as doorkeepers, keepers of the gates, porters, and Levites (Ps 84; 1 Chr 9:19-29; Num 3:27-39). The implications of their multi-faceted ministry for the deacons and deaconesses in the twenty-first century are to be responsible for opening and securing the church doors, organize their work and divide it among themselves, work with the treasury, keep inventory of supplies, equipment, and sacred vessels used in various services, and make sure that the church is left in order after each service. Part III consists of the following chapters:

CHAPTER 12

Election Process

When the seven deacons were elected to serve the first century Christian church, according to Acts 6:1-6, the twelve apostles called the "multitude of the disciples" together to explain to them the problem concerning the complaints of the widows about the daily distribution of food. The *SDA Bible Commentary* says,

> By "the multitude of the disciples" it is not to be supposed that every individual Christian in Jerusalem and its environs had to be gathered to a meeting, but that a special meeting was called, to which all came who could, and at which the apostles presented the problem and their plan. From this procedure in a single central place there naturally arose the representative form of church government.[1]

If the commentary is correct, "all came who could," then this meeting fell short of a representative form of church government in that those who were present did not necessarily represent an equitable ratio to membership formula as required by such governance. The representative form of church government was previously established by God during the time of Moses, according to the counsel of his father-in-law, Jethro, and was followed by the apostles at this meeting. Addressing the election of the seven deacons, Ellen G. White stated, "The same principles of piety and justice that were to guide the rulers among God's people in the time of Moses and David, were to be followed by those given the oversight of the newly organized church of God in the gospel dispensation."[2] She further added, "Summoning a meeting of the believers, the apostles were led by the Holy Spirit to outline a plan for the better organization of all the working forces of

---

[1]"Called the multitude," *SDA Bible Commentary*, 6:189.

[2]Ellen White, *The Acts of the Apostles*, 95.

the church."[3] She continued to explain:

> When dissension arose in a local church, as later it did arise in
> Antioch and elsewhere, and the believers were unable to
> come to an agreement among themselves, such matters were
> not permitted to create a division in the church, but were
> referred to a general council of the entire body of believers,
> made up of appointed delegates from the various local
> churches, with the apostles and elders in positions of leading
> responsibility. Thus the efforts of Satan to attack the church
> in isolated places were met by concerted action on the part of
> all, and the plans of the enemy to disrupt and destroy were
> thwarted.[4]

From these statements, it can be concluded that the meeting held to
elect the seven deacons was attended by a predetermined number of
delegates that represented the entire body of believers and not just
those who could come.

This representative form of government is still being used by the
Seventh-day Adventist church today in its process of electing church
officers, including deacons and deaconesses. The process is briefly
described as follows: the church membership elects a large committee
which is responsible for electing a nominating committee, which in
turn recommends to the church membership individuals to serve as
church officers. If the majority of the church members vote to accept
the nominating committee's recommendations, those individuals will
serve as officers of the church for one term, consisting of one or two
years. These individuals may be re-elected to serve additional terms for
as long as the church sees fit.

It is important to note, however, that the caliber of individuals
elected to serve as officers of the church, to a large degree, depends
upon the caliber of people that serve on the large committee and
nominating committee. Perhaps a more accurate statement would be
that it depends upon the spiritual condition of the membership, since

---

[3]Ibid., 89.

[4]Ibid., 96.

the process begins and ends with them. Nonetheless, the process is God inspired, although the outcome is sometimes flawed.

One of the flaws that must be avoided when electing individuals to serve as deacons and deaconesses is knowingly electing people to serve in these offices that do not meet the qualifications. Sometimes unqualified individuals are given a chance to see how they will work out in hopes of encouraging them to attend church regularly or to feel needed. Hiebert addresses this practice by saying,

> In 1 Timothy 3:10 Paul mentioned the testing of persons for appointment to the office of deacon. The meaning is not that they should be given a trial appointment as deacon, but rather that the church should constantly be examining and testing the members of the congregation, so that whenever the need for selecting deacons arises, they will know what members are qualified for appointment.[5]

Howard B. Foshee says, "Churches are often tempted to lower the spiritual qualifications at deacon election time. A church should never fall to this temptation. God in his divine wisdom set the qualifications high because the work of the deacon is spiritual in its nature and requires men who are mature Christians."[6]

The implication for the deacons and deaconesses of the Seventh-day Adventist church is that church members who sense that God is calling them to the ministry of deacon and deaconess should inform the head deacon, head deaconess, or pastor of their conviction and their desire to serve. The head deacon and head deaconess should take these individuals through a training program that should be conducted at least once a year, and allow them to work alongside the deacons and deaconesses as deacons/deaconesses in-training so that they can also receive some hands-on experience. The head deacon and head deaconess should also be observant of church members that show potential of serving as deacons and deaconesses; and through much prayer and guidance from God, recruit them to be trained along with

---

[5]Hiebert, 154.

[6]Howard B. Foshee, *Now That You're a Deacon* (Nashville: Broadman & Holman, 1975), 43.

the above mentioned group. By doing this, the church would have a pool of qualified individuals to elect to serve as needed—either at the beginning of a new term, or to add to those currently serving.

CHAPTER 13

Qualifications

In 1 Tim 3:8-13, the Apostle Paul presented the qualifications of deacons. He wrote,

> Likewise must the deacons be grave, not doubletongued, not given to much wine, not greedy of filthy lucre; Holding the mystery of the faith in a pure conscience. And let these also first be proved; then let them use the office of a deacon, being found blameless. Even so must their wives be grave, not slanderers, sober, faithful in all things. Let the deacons be the husbands of one wife, ruling their children and their own houses well. For they that have used the office of a deacon well purchase to themselves a good degree, and great boldness in the faith which is in Christ Jesus.

The word "grave" comes from the Greek word σεμνός, which means to be "worthy of honor," or "dignified."[7] The implication of this for deacons and deaconesses of the Seventh-day Adventist church is that they are to carry themselves in such a way that they earn the respect of others, including church members, residents of their community, people with whom they work, their colleagues in ministry, and members of their own family. By gaining the respect of others, these officers will be in a better position to minister to them and influence them to accept the Christian faith.

To be doubletongued means "saying a thing to one person and giving a different view of it to another."[8] Being doubletongued is the result of being unstable and double minded. According to Jas 1:8, "A double minded man is unstable in all his ways." In her Beatitudes for deacons, Riley says, "Blessed is the deacon who is not 'doubled-tongued' and will not engage in gossip. Cheap talk will defile you.

[7]"Grave," *SDA Bible Commentary*, 7:299.

[8]W. E. Vine, *Expository Dictionary of New Testament Words* (1952), s.v. "Doubletongued."

Shun unsavory conversations. Talk your Church and Pastor Up, and not Down, and always protect their image, for righteous sake."[9] Foshee, quotes Walter A. Bennett, Jr., a pastor and denominational leader who said, "'Church activities are much more successful when deacons give them verbal endorsement and active participation. One deacon with an indifferent attitude toward a revival or visitation campaign can weaken the effectiveness of his entire group.'"[10]

The injunction to be "not given to much wine" can be rather difficult to understand whether we believe Paul was referring to unfermented wine (grape juice) or fermented wine (intoxicating beverage). The *SDA Bible Commentary* presents the dilemma as following,

> Some hold that Paul here speaks of unfermented wine—grape juice—because for him to speak otherwise would place him in conflict with his declaration against defiling the body (see on I Cor. 6:19; 10:31), and contrary to the general teaching of the Bible regarding intoxicating drink (see on Prov. 20:1; 23:29-32). Others hold that Paul here permits a temperate use of ordinary wine. They declare that if he were speaking of grape juice he would not need to warn the deacons against drinking "much" of it, and would have no valid basis for forbidding the elders to drink it at all. The passage is admittedly difficult.[11]

The difficulty in understanding this injunction is lessened, however, by translating the Greek phrase μὴ οἴνῳ πολλῷ προσέχοντας to mean, "be not addicted to much wine"[12] instead of "be not given to much wine." This translation places the emphasis or warning against being addicted to wine (alcoholism) rather than a warning about the amount of wine that one can consume. If Paul was instructing deacons

---

[9]Riley, 145.

[10]Foshee, 51.

[11]"Wine," *SDA Bible Commentary*, 7:299.

[12]Jay P. Green, Sr., gen. ed. and trans., *The Interlinear Bible*, 2nd ed. (Peabody, MA: Hendrickson Publishers, 1986).

not to be addicted to wine, then the only sure way to prevent addiction is abstinence, which is in harmony with his declaration against defiling the body, and with the general teaching of the Bible regarding intoxicating drink. Anne M. Fletcher quotes a woman she refers to as Karen M. who said, "'It's not so much the frequency of drinking but how it affects your life when you do.'"[13] Therefore, I favor the interpretation "be not addicted to much wine," and believe that the apostle Paul was advocating abstinence from fermented wine.

Robert E. Naylor comments on Paul's counsel to both the bishop and the deacon concerning this issue of wine. In verse three of this same chapter, Paul says that a bishop must be "not given to wine." Whereas in verse eight, he says that a deacon must be "not given to much wine." Naylor says,

> Many brethren have taken a great deal of comfort from the fact that while the preacher is not to use wine, the deacon is simply not to use much wine. They would interpret that to provide the deacon with a certain liberty in the matter of alcoholic drink, as long as it is not done, as some say, to excess. There is no real ground for believing that a double standard is created by the Scriptures. A deacon has a responsibility towards God in the matter of alcoholic drink. A fair examination of the Bible indicates that a man who is to be useful in accepting a vow that makes him a servant of the church for the rest of his life must leave intoxicating drink and even the appearance of it out of his life.[14]

Naylor even takes it a step further and rightly so, by stating, "Abstaining from alcoholic drink is not quite enough for the deacon. He is to have nothing to do with the liquor traffic. A man that in some fashion profits from the debaucheries of men is not only a poor deacon but a poor church member. A man should not be selected as a

---

[13]Anne M. Fletcher, *Sober for Good: New Solutions for Drinking Problems---Advice from Those Who Have Succeeded* (New York: Houghton Mifflin Company, 2001), 26.

[14]Robert E. Naylor, *The Baptist Deacon* (Nashville: Broadman & Holman, 1955), 23.

deacon in any church that in any wise is engaged in the sale of liquors."[15]

Naylor's statements succinctly express the implication of this qualification for deacons and deaconesses of the Seventh-day Adventist church—abstain from alcoholic drink and the trafficking of such. This admonition is in harmony with the Seventh-day Adventist baptismal vows, which all members are to adhere to. Number ten of the thirteen vows states,

> Do you believe that your body is the temple of the Holy Spirit; and will you honor God by caring for it, avoiding the use of that which is harmful, abstaining from all unclean foods; from the use, manufacture, or sale of alcoholic beverages; the use, manufacture, or sale of tobacco in any of its forms for human consumption; and from the misuse of or trafficking in narcotics or other drugs?[16]

The next qualification listed for deacons is that they be "not greedy of filthy lucre." They were not to accept ill gotten gain, bribes, or show favor to individuals or to a certain group(s) in the church for personal gain. They were to remain fair and objective in carrying out their responsibilities, otherwise they would forfeit the trust of those whom they were called to serve. This command also warned against taking advantage of people.

The implication of this for deacons and deaconesses of the Seventh-day Adventist church in the twenty-first century is that they see the importance of gaining and maintaining the respect and trust of church members in a post-modern era when everyone and everything is suspect.

"Holding the mystery of the faith in a pure conscience" is the next qualification. According to Vine, the Greek word for mystery, μυστήριον, means "that which is known to the initiated. In the NT it denotes not the mysterious (as with the Eng. word), but that which, being outside the range of unassisted natural apprehension, can be

---

[15]Ibid.

[16]General Conference of Seventh-day Adventists, *Church Manual*, 33.

made known only by Divine revelation, and is made known in a manner and at a time appointed by God, and to those only who are illumined by His Spirit."[17]

This implies that deacons and deaconesses are to have such a connection with God that He will give them divine revelations about His Word, as they spend quality time in prayer and the study of God's Word.

Another one of Riley's Beatitudes can be applied to the deacons and deaconesses of the Seventh-day Adventist church. It says,

> BLESSED IS THE DEACON who considers it not robbery to sacrifice time to study God's Word. He too needs to be able to "rightly divide the Word of Truth." Attending Sunday Church School [Sabbath Church School] or teaching a Sunday School Class [Sabbath School Class], will not only sharpen his own spiritual knowledge, but will enhance his role as a Bible believing church leader. He should also better prepare himself for this ever challenging role, by keeping abreast with other good spiritual informative literature.[18]

The apostle Paul continued his list by stating, "Let these also first be proved; then let them use the office of a deacon, being found blameless" (1 Tim 3:10). Evidently, the prospective deacons were scrutinized by the church to see if they possessed a godly character, sound judgment, and had the potential to develop all of the qualifications Paul listed. All areas of their lives were investigated to see if they were fit to hold this sacred office. This insured that the right caliber of persons was being chosen to serve the church.

Webb presents some implications of this admonition for deacons and deaconesses of the Seventh-day Adventist church. He states,

> Many churches also require prospective deacons to be church members for a specific period of time. This gives church members a more adequate opportunity to become familiar with their qualifications for deacon service. This time also

---

[17]Vine, s.v. "Mystery."

[18]Riley, 144-145.

gives prospective deacons an opportunity to become familiar with the nature and style of the church and how deacons minister in it. A one-year requirement is most common, but some churches require as little as six months and others as much as two years.[19]

Webb continues to say,

> Churches often require some external signs of commitment to the church. Most frequently cited is regular participation in church programs such as Sunday School [Sabbath School], Church Training, Sunday worship services [Sabbath worship services], and midweek prayer service. Deacons are often expected to be tithers, giving 10 percent or more of their income through the church budget. A church may also require regular deacons' meeting attendance and participation in specific training for deacon ministry.[20]

The implication for the Seventh-day Adventist church in the twenty-first century is to not take the election of deacons and deaconesses lightly. Serious thought and prayer must take place before putting a person in this office. Also, those who feel that they are being rushed into office before they are ready to assume such awesome responsibilities should decline. They may even request to be placed in a training capacity until they are confident that God is directing them to serve in this office.

Ellen G. White said, "It would be well for all our ministers to give heed to these words and not to hurry men into office without due consideration and much prayer that God would designate by His Holy Spirit whom He will accept."[21] Although White directed her comment to the election of elders, the same principle is applicable when electing deacons and deaconesses.

---

[19]Webb, *Deacons: Servant Models in the* Church, 13.

[20]Ibid., 13-14.

[21]Ellen G. White, *Testimonies for the Church*, vol. 5 (Boise, ID: Pacific Press, 1948), 617.

The final items on Paul's list of qualifications of deacons are: "Even so must their wives be grave, not slanderers, sober, faithful in all things. Let the deacons be the husbands of one wife, ruling their children and their own houses well" (1 Tim 3:11-12).

It was concluded in chapter 3 that the best translation for the word "wives" is "women," meaning "women deacons." Therefore, Paul held the women deacons accountable to the same qualifications as the male deacons. These women were to conduct themselves with dignity, not find fault to criticize others, abstain from intoxicating drinks, and be faithful in all things. Both male and female deacons were to train their children to be obedient, respectful, and how to behave at home, in public, and at church.

The admonition that deacons were to be the husband of one wife is the same admonition given to bishops in 1 Tim 3:2. The *SDA Bible Commentary* only comments on this phrase as it applies to the bishop. It offers four explanations and the arguments in favor of and against each of them. After considering them, I conclude that the admonition given to the deacons did not mean that men had to be married in order to hold this office. It simply meant that if they were married, they could only have one wife at a time. This was a safe guard against polygamy. This also applied to men who divorced their wives on non-biblical grounds and remarried. However, there is still a question about the eligibility of those who divorced their wives on biblical grounds and remarried since, according to the *SDA Bible Commentary*, "even as the Jews recognized the most trivial grounds for divorce (see Matt 5:32), some of the early Christians were excusing divorce for causes other than adultery (see Matt 19:8, 9). A bishop divorced for any reason would be handicapped as a spiritual leader."[22] If this argument was true concerning the election of bishops, it is possible that it applied to deacons as well. However, the commentary confirms that "nowhere in Scripture is remarriage after the death of a first spouse condemned, nor is it considered detrimental to spiritual leadership."[23]

Ed Glasscock's position addresses the statements in 1 Tim 2:3, 12 that bishops and deacons are to be the husbands of one wife. He

---

[22]"One Wife," *SDA Bible Commentary*, 7:298.

[23]Ibid.

suggests that "it is more probable that Paul was concerned not so much with a man's marital status as he was with his character."[24] After a number of arguments, Glasscock bases his position on an alternate interpretation of "husband of one wife." He states,

> The translation "husband of one wife" is not the best understanding of the Greek phrase μᾶς γυναικὸς ἄνδρα, but that it should be translated "a man of one woman" or 'a one-woman man.' This understanding emphasizes the character of the man rather than his marital status. Thus even a single man or a man who has been married only once must demonstrate that he is not a "playboy" or flirtatious, but that he is stable and mature in character toward his wife or other females. A man who demonstrates a character of loyalty and trustworthiness in such personal relationships is qualified in this area. He, being a one-woman type man, can be placed in this high position and trusted to deal in maturity and with discretion in a situation involving female members. This view shifts the emphasis away from an event that took place in a man's life before his conversion and properly concentrates on the character and quality of his life at the time of his consideration for this high office.[25]

Glasscock's position challenges the traditional interpretation of this passage. However, I believe that there is sufficient evidence that his position may be correct. At least it is worth our consideration. Echlin is also in agreement with Glasscock. He says, "Recently it has been suggested that the famous Pauline strictures against remarriage may mean that ministers should be totally loyal to their wives."[26]

The implication of this qualification for the deacons and deaconesses of the Seventh-day Adventist church is that they are to set a godly example in their home, be faithful to their spouse if they

---

[24]Ed Glasscock, "'The Husband of One Wife' Requirement in 1 Timothy 3:2," *Bibliotheca Sacra* 140 (July-September 1983): 246.

[25]Ibid., 249.

[26]Echlin, 11.

are married, do not be flirtatious with the opposite sex, and train their children to be obedient.

Ellen G. White also stressed the importance of the family of church officers. She counseled,

> The family of the one suggested for office should be considered. Are they in subjection? Can the man rule his own house with honor? What character have his children? Will they do honor to the father's influence? If he has no tact, wisdom, or power of godliness at home in managing his own family, it is safe to conclude that the same defects will be carried into the church, and the same unsanctified management will be seen there.[27]

White was again addressing the hasty election of elders. However, this is also true in the case of deacons and deaconesses.

An example of how important it is for the family members of deacons and deaconesses to be converted and have a godly influence in the church can be seen from this situation that White wrote about in 1862. She addressed an issue concerning the "power of example" when the children of a deacon wore immodest clothing. The example of the deacon's children caused the other children in the church to question their parents on why they could not wear what the deacon's children were wearing. The article of clothing was called hoops. White described hoops as a shame and indecent. She said, "Children urge the example of other children, whose parents are Sabbathkeepers. Brother A is a deacon of the church. His children wear hoops, and why is it any worse for me to wear them than it is for them?"[28] She continued to stress the importance of influence by saying, "Those who by their example furnish unconsecrated professors with arguments against those who would be peculiar, are laying a cause of stumbling in the way of the weak; they must render an account to God for their example."[29]

---

[27]Ellen White, *Testimonies for the Church*, 5:618.

[28]Ibid., 1:276.

[29]Ibid.

It is difficult for deacons and deaconesses to teach others to obey God's Word and the standards of the church when their children and/or spouse disregard them. Other members who want to disregard these standards will use the example of the deacon's family as an excuse.

CHAPTER 14

Solving Problems and Nurturing the Membership

It has been established that the deacons of the first century Christian church ministered to the members that joined the church by solving problems and nurturing them. Therefore, the implication is that the deacons and deaconesses of the Seventh-day Adventist church in the twenty-first century must be involved in preparing the church to welcome new members into its ranks, and nurture them.

Ellen G. White stated that "God's Spirit convicts sinners of the truth, and He places them in the arms of the church. The ministers may do their part, but they can never perform the work that the church should do. God requires His church to nurse those who are young in faith and experience."[30] This statement indicates that baptizing people into the church is not the end of the process of soul winning. Church members have a responsibility to nurture, train, and assimilate the new members into the church. It must be carefully noted that this responsibility rests upon the entire church membership and not solely on the pastor. In following the biblical model as outlined in the book of Acts, the deacons and deaconesses have an important role to play in accomplishing this task.

For further implications of the ministry of deacons in the first century Christian church for deacons and deaconesses of the Seventh-day Adventist church, I direct your attention to Ellen G. White's inspired account of the election of the seven deacons in the first century Christian church:

> The church accordingly selected seven men full of faith and the wisdom of the Spirit of God, to attend to the business pertaining to the cause. Stephen was chosen first: he was a Jew by birth and religion, but spoke the Greek language, and was conversant with the customs and manners of the Greeks.

---

[30]Ellen G. White, *Evangelism* (1946; repr., Hagerstown: Review and Herald Publishing Assn., 1970), 352.

He was therefore considered the most proper person to stand at the head and have supervision of the disbursement of the funds appropriated to the widows, orphans, and the worthy poor. This selection met the minds of all, and the dissatisfaction and murmuring were quieted.

The seven chosen men were solemnly set apart for their duties by prayer and the laying on of hands. Those who were thus ordained were not thereby excluded from teaching the faith. On the contrary, it is recorded that "Stephen, full of faith and power, did great wonders and miracles among the people." They were fully qualified to instruct in the truth. They were also men of calm judgment and discretion, well calculated to deal with difficult cases of trial, of murmuring or jealousy.

This choosing of men to transact the business of the church, so that the apostles could be left free for their special work of teaching the truth, was greatly blessed of God. The church advanced in numbers and strength. "And the word of God increased; and the number of the disciples multiplied in Jerusalem greatly; and a great company of the priests were obedient to the faith."

It is necessary that the same order and system should be maintained in the church now as in the days of the apostles. The prosperity of the cause depends very largely upon its various departments being conducted by men of ability, who are qualified for their positions. Those who are chosen of God to be leaders in the cause of God, having the general oversight of the spiritual interest of the church, should be relieved, as far as possible, from cares and perplexities of a temporal nature. Those whom God has called to minister in word and doctrine should have time for meditation, prayer, and study of the Scriptures. Their clear spiritual discernment is dimmed by entering into the lesser details of business and dealing with the various temperaments of those who meet together in church capacity.[31]

---

[31]Ellen White, *The Story of Redemption*, 260-261.

From this account, I propose four implications of the ministry of the deacons in the first century Christian church that can be applied to the ministry of deacons and deaconesses of the Seventh-day Adventist church as it relates to solving problems and nurturing the membership. First of all, it is important to note the qualities of Stephen, who was elected to serve as the head deacon. Although he was a Jew, he spoke the Greek language and was familiar with Greek culture. Therefore, Stephen was capable of identifying with and relating to both of the groups that were in contention—the Grecians or Hellenistic Christians and the Hebrews or Palestinian Jewish converts. The implication is that the Seventh-day Adventist church must elect men and women to serve as deacons and deaconesses who show evidence of being capable of identifying with and relating to the various groups that make up the church membership. The membership of the church in the twenty-first century is divided by culture, ethnicity, complexion, race, socioeconomic status, age, education, gender, liturgy, music, theology, dress, diet, etc. Deacons and deaconesses must be skilled in building relationships across these divides if they are to have a positive influence among the membership.

To emphasize the importance of this point, allow me to share one of the most humbling experiences that I have had in pastoral ministry. I was very polished and fresh out of the seminary when this incident occurred. I was visiting with a family whose teenage daughter had become pregnant. As I spoke with the daughter, she did not respond to me verbally. Finally, her mother said, "don't you hear the pastor talking to you? Why don't you say something?" With tears in her eyes, the daughter responded by saying, "Momma, I don't understand a thing that he's saying." Naturally, I thought that the problem was with her. In fact, I thought that all of the members who could not understand me had problems. But God gave me a wake-up call one day while I was on vacation in Florida. I saw a bumper sticker on a pickup truck that read, "We don't care how you use to do it up north, you're down here now!" Finally, a light bulb came on in my head. It was beginning to click—I wasn't speaking the language of the people. If I had taken my head deacon or deaconess on that visit with me, things would have probably turned out differently. They knew that teenage girl from birth. They had known her parents for years. Perhaps they were classmates or buddies growing up in the same community. That girl would have understood everything that the deacon and deaconess would have said. They spoke her language.

After Stephen and the other deacons were elected to serve the church, the dissatisfaction and murmuring ceased between the Grecians and Hebrews. Therefore, the second implication is that the church must elect men and women to serve as deacons and deaconesses who have skills in resolving conflicts. These officers are to recognize that they have been called as conflict managers, social workers, and spiritual counselors. Their primary responsibility is to restore unity and peace in the church when the members begin to murmur. In other words; they are "problem solvers."[32]

The deacons of the first century Christian church were able to teach the Word of God. They were also calm, and had discernment. Therefore, the third implication is that the deacons and deaconesses of the Seventh-day Adventist church must be qualified to instruct others in the Word of God, have self control, and be able to reason from cause to effect.

We are further told that God greatly blessed the first century Christian church by increasing its membership. This was due to the deacons being willing to take care of the social needs and relational problems of the membership and allowing the apostles to focus on their primary calling of teaching the Word of God. Therefore, the fourth and final implication is that the Seventh-day Adventist church in the twenty-first century will grow spiritually and numerically when the men and women that are elected to serve as deacons and deaconesses follow the same model of taking care of the social needs and relational problems of the membership and allowing the pastor and elders to focus on their primary calling of teaching God's Word, meditating, praying, and studying the Scriptures.

Barnett presents a list of functions for deacons to carry out among the church membership. My conviction is that it is also the deaconesses' responsibility to carry out these functions. These functions are in harmony with the principles set forth in the first century Christian church for the work of deacons, and should be carried out by the deacons and deaconesses of the Seventh-day Adventist church in the twenty-first century. Barnett says,

_____

[32]Vincent White, xviii, xvii.

The following are functions which ordinarily are primarily focused upon ministry to the Church's own people and illustrate the kinds of things they might encompass:

1. To visit the sick and the shut-ins.
2. To care for and about the parish's poor.
3. To coordinate a program for visiting and integrating newcomers.
4. To visit prospects for entering [joining] the Church.
5. To instruct adults in the precatechumenate, catechumenate, and postbaptismal catechesis. [Adapted for Seventh-day Adventists—To instruct adults in Bible studies in preparation for baptism, fundamental beliefs of the church, and postbaptismal Bible studies/new believers class].
6. To teach the children of the church.
7. To lead small study/prayer/sharing groups.
8. To organize and head groups and activities to serve special needs within the Christian community.
9. To train acolytes or altar servers. [Adapted for Seventh-day Adventists—To establish and train a group of youth to serve as junior deacons and deaconesses].
10. To work with student groups.
11. To instruct parents and godparents for baptisms. [Adapted for Seventh-day Adventists—To instruct parents and guardians for baby/child dedications].
12. To lead parish discussion groups.
13. To organize and coordinate retreats, workshops, and similar activities.
14. To coordinate ushers or "parish hosts."
15. To develop youth programs and activities. [Adapted for Seventh-day Adventists—To serve as sponsors and advisors to the youth department].
16. To counsel those with problems.
17. To coordinate and train lectors. [Adapted for Seventh-day Adventists—To coordinate and train deacons and deaconesses to lead out in mid-week prayer meetings and participate on platform during worship services].

18. To assume responsibility for some aspect of parish or diocesan administration.[33]

As the Seventh-day Adventist church in the twenty-first century returns to the biblical model of the first century Christian church and allows its deacons and deaconesses to solve problems and nurture the membership, it will experience greater results.

---

[33]Barnett, 184.

CHAPTER 15

Proclaiming the Gospel
and Winning Souls

The impact that the deacons made in the early church was astounding—"The word of God increased; and the number of the disciples multiplied in Jerusalem greatly" (Acts 6:7). Dockery states that "the selection of the seven started the church on its world evangelism mission."[34]

With great insight, Ellen G. White attributed this growth experience to the work of the deacons. She stated,

> This ingathering of souls was due both to the greater freedom secured by the apostles and the zeal and power shown by the seven deacons. The fact that these brethren had been ordained for the special work of looking after the needs of the poor, did not exclude them from teaching the faith. On the contrary, they were fully qualified to instruct others in the truth, and they engaged in the work with great earnestness and success.[35]

These statements indicate that in addition to addressing the physical needs of the poor, the deacons of the early church proclaimed the gospel and won converts to the church, as did the apostles.

The Book of Acts gives us undisputable evidence of this fact as it portrays the ministry of Philip and Stephen in particular. Although there is no biblical record that proves that the other deacons proclaimed the gospel and won converts, neither is there any record that proves that they did not. According to 1 Tim 3:9, one of the qualifications necessary to serve as a deacon is to hold the mystery of the faith in a pure conscience. This includes being "a well-informed

---

[34]Dockery, 424.

[35]Ellen White, *The Acts of the Apostles*, 90.

Bible student."[36] This would suggest that all of the deacons were expected to share their faith verbally.

The deacon Philip is portrayed as being effective as both an evangelist and as a Bible worker. He is even referred to as an evangelist in Acts 21:8. "And the next day we that were of Paul's company departed, and came unto Caesarea: and we entered into the house of Philip the evangelist, which was one of the seven; and abode with him."

As an evangelist, Philip conducted a public evangelistic meeting in the city of Samaria with tremendous success. The story is recorded as following:

> Then Philip went down to the city of Samaria, and preached Christ unto them. And the people with one accord gave heed unto those things which Philip spake, hearing and seeing the miracles which he did. For unclean spirits, crying with loud voice, came out of many that were possessed with them: and many taken with palsies, and that were lame, were healed. And there was great joy in that city (Acts 8:5-8).

According to Ellen G. White, God used Philip's evangelistic work in Samaria to help the apostles to understand Jesus' prediction concerning their witnessing. She said, "Philip's work in Samaria was marked with great success, and, thus encouraged, he sent to Jerusalem for help. The apostles now perceived more fully the meaning of the words of Christ, 'Ye shall be witnesses unto Me both in Jerusalem, and in all Judea, and in Samaria, and unto the uttermost part of the earth.' Acts 1:8."[37]

Not only was Philip an evangelist with the skills to conduct a public meeting, he also had the skills to teach the Scriptures to a one-person audience. After completing the meeting in Samaria, Philip was instructed by the angel of the Lord to go into the desert of Gaza. When he arrived there, he met an Ethiopian eunuch who was reading the Scriptures. Philip explained the Scriptures to him, and baptized him (Acts 8:34-38).

---

[36]"Faith," *SDA Bible Commentary*, 7:299-300.

[37]Ellen White, *The Acts of the Apostles*, 107.

Another example of a deacon that won converts to the church is Stephen. According to Ellen G. White's description of him, we could consider Stephen the head deacon of the early church. White said, "Stephen was chosen first; he was a Jew by birth and religion, but spoke the Greek language, and was conversant with the customs and manners of the Greeks. He was therefore considered the most proper person to stand at the head and have supervision of the disbursement of the funds appropriated to the widows, orphans, and the worthy poor."[38]

Acts 6:8 gives this account of Stephen, "And Stephen, full of faith and power, did great wonders and miracles among the people." Unfortunately Stephen received great opposition because of his work and was stoned to death (Acts 7:58-60. However, Saul witnessed the courage of Stephen and was convicted. Ellen G. White shared this account,

> His [Stephen's] death was a sore trial to the church, but it resulted in the conviction of Saul, who could not efface from his memory the faith and constancy of the martyr, and the glory that had rested on his countenance. For a time he [Saul] was a mighty instrument in the hands of Satan. But soon this relentless persecutor was to be employed in building up the church that he was now tearing down. A Mightier than Satan had chosen Saul to take the place of the martyred Stephen, to preach and suffer for His name, and to spread far and wide the tidings of salvation through His blood.[39]

Dockery makes a similar observation concerning Stephen's death and Saul's conviction. He says, "Saul became a prime mover in the new persecution of the church because he was zealous for the traditions of his fathers (Gal. 1:13). He began to devastate the churches. Luke, however, wants us to see that out of a seeming tragedy there was advance in the Christian mission. Out of Stephen came Saul (hereafter referred to as Paul)."[40] Therefore, not only did

---

[38]Ellen White, *The Story of Redemption*, 260.

[39]Ellen White, *The Acts of the Apostles*, 101-102.

[40]Dockery, 426.

Stephen witness by his life and his words, but he also witnessed by his death.

In addition to these two stalwart male deacons—Philip and Stephen—there were also female deacons or deaconesses that were instrumental in instructing others and winning converts to the church. As previously stated, Schaff proposed that Priscilla, whom Paul mentioned along with Phoebe, was also a deaconess.[41] Christopher Wordworth agrees with Schaff and says, "From the position of her name immediately after Phoebe the Deaconess, and before her husband and all the other Roman Christians [Rom 16], it may be inferred, that Priscilla also was appointed by St. Paul to do some special work, like that of a Deaconess, in the Church."[42] However, due to the lack of definitive evidence, Jane Marie Bancroft states that we have "no means of knowing" if Priscilla and the other women mentioned by Paul in Rom 16 were deaconesses.[43] I am inclined to agree with Cecilia Robinson—to let Priscilla's work speak for her. Robinson says, "It was women such as Phoebe and Priscilla who created the ideal of the female diaconate. Whether or no they received the name as an official title matters but little; they certainly 'executed the office' of a Deaconess, and bore splendid testimony to the value of a ministry of women."[44] Therefore, based upon the Scriptures, Priscilla was a powerful example of one who instructed others in the truth.

Priscilla and her husband Aquila instructed Apollos, a prominent leader of the early church, in the Word of God. Sensing that Apollos' understanding was limited to the teaching of John the Baptist, Priscilla and Aquila "took him unto them, and expounded unto him the way of God more perfectly" (Acts 18:26). According to the *SDA Bible*

---

[41]Schaff, 1:500-501.

[42]Christopher Wordsworth, *The New Testament of Our Lord and Saviour Jesus Christ* (1923; repr., Charleston, SC: BiblioLife, LLC, 2009), 130.

[43]Jane Marie Bancroft, *Deaconesses in Europe and Their Lessons for America* (1890; repr., Charleston, SC: BiblioBazaar, LLC, 2008), 18.

[44]Cecilia Robinson, *The Ministry of Deaconesses* (1898; repr., Charleston, SC: BiblioBazaar, LLC, 2008), 12.

Commentary, the teaching that Apollos received from Priscilla and Aquila "would include the doctrine of salvation by grace, justification by faith, the gift of the Holy Spirit after conversion and baptism, and the meaning and necessity of the Lord's Supper."[45] This is evident that Priscilla was knowledgeable of the Scriptures and apt to teach.

To further describe how involved she was in instructing others in the truth, the commentary states: "It would doubtless follow, as in the case of the twelve men discussed in [Acts] ch. 19:1-7, that Apollos, who formerly knew only John's baptism, would be rebaptized into 'the name of the Lord Jesus.' She evidently took an active part in instructing Apollos, indicating that she was a woman of great power and zeal among the Christians."[46] Although it may not be conclusive that Priscilla was a deaconess, it is certain that she proclaimed the gospel and won souls to the Lord.

Edmond Cullinan indicates that Phoebe may have also engaged in proclaiming the gospel and winning souls. He states that "her ministry may not have corresponded exactly to that of later deaconesses; indeed it may have been more extensive, particularly in terms of preaching and teaching which were particular concerns of St. Paul."[47]

Regarding those deaconesses who were not in the forefront as were Priscilla and Phoebe, but worked in a more subtle way; Schaff noted the tactful manner in which they used their humanitarian role as an opportunity to teach others the truth and win converts to the church. Concerning the office of deaconess, he said,

> It opened to pious women and virgins, and chiefly to widows, a suitable field for the regular official exercise of their peculiar gifts of self-denying charity and devotion to the welfare of the church. Through it they could carry the light and comfort of the gospel into the most private and delicate relations of

---

[45]"Way of God," *SDA Bible Commentary*, 6:369.

[46]Ibid.

[47]Edmond Cullinan, "Women and the Diaconate," *Worship* 70, no. 3 (May 1996): 261.

domestic life, without at all overstepping their natural sphere.[48]

Citing Clement of Alexandria, Vyhmeister writes of another subtle way in which these women ministered: "'But the apostles in conformity with their ministry concentrated on undistracted preaching, and took their wives around as Christian sisters rather than spouses, to be their fellow-ministers ["fellow deacons"] in relation to housewives, through whom the Lord's teaching penetrated into the women's quarters without scandal.'"[49]

The female deacons or deaconesses ministered by using the gifts that God gave them within the context of their own unique personalities and circumstances, as did the male deacons. Some were in the forefront in instructing others in the truth while others worked subtly behind the scenes. Both were effective in their ministry.

The implication of the deacons and deaconesses in the first century Christian church proclaiming the gospel and winning souls for the deacons and deaconesses of the Seventh-day Adventist church in the twenty-first century is that there is a potential for an explosion of new members added to the church. They can win souls by conducting public meetings—tent meetings, hall meetings, church meetings, and prophecy seminars. They can serve as Bible workers in meetings conducted by their pastors, which would reduce the expense of hiring outside Bible workers. And since the deacons and deaconesses would remain at their local church, they could continue to visit and study with the people who did not decide to join the church when the meeting ended. They would be more effective in nurturing and assimilating the new members into church-life because of the relationship they would have built with them throughout the course of the meetings. They could train those newly baptized members how to share their faith with their family and friends, thus, they would become soul-winners also.

Barnett presents a list of practical ministries to be conducted by deacons and deaconesses that would address many of the social needs

---

[48]Schaff, 1:500.

[49]Vyhmeister, "The Ministry of the Deaconess," 18.

found in all communities. These ministries could serve as an entering wedge for presenting the gospel, once the people's confidence has been won.

1. To help and befriend the powerless who are in need: prisoners, the poor, the rejected.
2. To counsel the troubled.
3. To work in referral programs to help those in crisis situations.
4. To lead or work in community action groups to effect social change.
5. To organize and promote community activities or programs to meet special needs: drug and alcohol dependencies, unwed parents, etc.
6. To work with juveniles and adults in hospitals, prisons, orphanages, half-way houses, and other institutions.
7. To serve youth in various educational and recreational programs.
8. To care for the needs of the elderly and disabled.
9. To visit the lonely and neglected, especially those in institutions.
10. To work with the handicapped.
11. To provide employment help to those leaving institutions, such as prisons, half-way houses, drug and alcohol treatment centers.[50]

Barnett also gives suggestions for ministries that could grow out of a deacon's and deaconess' work situation. In fact, the deacons and deaconesses could identify other church members that work in these areas and organize ministry teams. Barnett states,

> The modern diaconate should serve to enable and encourage those in varied occupations and life situations to develop special ministries of service, though these do not lend themselves to precise categories. Some of these ministries would be natural outgrowths of occupational vocations. A nurse or a lawyer might give part of his or her time to service in a free clinic on a regular and continuing basis. Such service,

---

[50]Barnett, 185.

enlightened and informed by the Spirit, is a diakonia of love and rises above the level of mere social service.

A teacher might offer special classes or personal instruction to children with learning problems. A salesperson could offer time and expertise to teach volunteers how to "sell" charitable organizations to prospective supporters to raise needed financial support.[51]

As the deacons and deaconesses of the Seventh-day Adventist church adopt the mind-set of being soul-winners, they will earnestly pray for opportunities to witness for Jesus and implement some of Barnett's suggestions. As they focus on their mission to spread the gospel, I believe that "the Lord [will add] to the church daily such as should be saved" (Acts 2:47).

---

[51]Ibid.

CHAPTER 16

The Sons of Korah as Doorkeepers

Psalm 84 is introduced with a superscription that reads, "To the chief Musician upon Gittith, A Psalm for the sons of Korah." The word "Gittith" is derived from the Hebrew word "Gath," which means wine press. This indicates that this psalm was sung with a joyful spirit. It may even suggest the manner in which the sons of Korah were to carry out their responsibilities in the Temple of God. They were to do it with joy. Commenting on this psalm, Charles Spurgeon said, "Sweeter than the joy of the wine press, is the joy of the holy assemblies of the Lord's house."[52]

The sons of Korah were the descendants of Korah who escaped God's punishment on their father for rebelling against Moses and Aaron (Num 16:1-35). They became leaders in the worship services at the temple of God. Their commitment to service is reflected in v. 10, which states, "For a day in thy courts is better than a thousand. I had rather be a doorkeeper in the house of my God, than to dwell in the tents of wickedness." This is in stark contrast to the attitude of their father Korah. Being servants in the house of God was these officers' ultimate reason for existence.

First Chronicles 9:19 tells us that the Sons of Korah became the keepers of the gates of the tabernacle: "And Shallum the son of Kore, the son of Ebiasaph, the son of Korah, and his brethren, of the house of his father, the Korahites, were over the work of the service, keepers of the gates of the tabernacle: and their fathers, being over the host of the Lord, were keepers of the entry." These men were chosen by David and Samuel because of their faithfulness (v. 22). The implication for the Seventh-day Adventist church in the twenty-first century is that it is to select persons that are committed and faithful to serve in the office of deacon and deaconess.

The sons of Korah lived in close proximity to the tabernacle. They lived on the north, south, east, and west sides so that they could

---

[52]Charles H. Spurgeon, *The Treasury of David* (McLean, VA: MacDonald Publishing Company, *n.d.*), 2:432.

keep a vigilant watch over it. They lived close to the tabernacle because it was their responsibility to open the doors every morning for worship. First Chronicles 9:27 says, "And they lodged round about the house of God, because the charge was upon them, and the opening thereof every morning pertained to them." The implications for deacons and deaconesses of the twenty-first century is that they should arrive at the church prior to the time for services so that they can open the doors and greet the worshipers as they enter. They should also, make the church accessible to those members that have a need to enter at times other than the weekly worship service.

According to 1 Chr 9:25, the sons of Korah were to take turns and rotate their duties from Sabbath to Sabbath. It reads, "And their brethren, which were in their villages, were to come after seven days from time to time with them." The implications of this for the deacons and deaconesses of the twenty-first century is that they should organize their work. They should divide their responsibilities among themselves so that the burden of the work is shared by all. This will prevent any one of them from being overworked.

The sons of Korah were also referred to as keepers of the gates (v. 19), porters (v. 22), and Levites (v. 26; Num 3:27-39). They were members of the Korahites and Kohathite tribes (v. 19; Num 16:1; 3:27). Some of them were over the treasuries (v. 26). Others were over the sacred vessels and instruments of the sanctuary. And others were in charge of the fine flour, wine, oil, frankincense, and spices (vv. 28-29). The implication of this for deacons and deaconesses of the twenty-first century is that their ministry is multifaceted. Their presence and influence are to be felt throughout the church. It is appropriate for some of them to work in the treasury department. Others may keep an inventory of the supplies, equipment, and vessels used in various services of the church. Some of them will make use of flour, oil, and wine in preparation for the ordinance of Holy Communion.

The sons of Korah were so committed to their charge that Ps 84:2 suggests that when they were not present at the Tabernacle, they desired to be there. The verse reads, "My soul longeth, yea, even fainteth for the courts of the Lord: my heart and my flesh crieth out for the living God." Primarily, this verse may be expressing David's longing to be present at the temple, since he wrote this psalm while in exile. Nonetheless, it describes how the sons of Korah should have felt about carrying out their responsibilities. The implication of this for the deacons and deaconesses of the twenty-first century is that they should love their work. It is not enough for them to simply be present in the flesh—doing their work mechanically. They must put their heart into their work if they are to be effective. David said, "My heart and my flesh crieth out for the living God."

David indicated that God will bless those who are committed in their service to Him. Ps 84:4 says, "Blessed are they that dwell in thy house: they will be still praising thee." Like the sons of Korah, deacons and deaconesses are the ones that dwell in God's house today. They have devoted their lives to the service of God's house. They dwell there in the sense that they are the ones who remain there after everyone else has gone. They see to it that God's house is left in order and that the sacred vessels used in the service are accounted for and put in their proper place. They assist the ushers in making sure that the church hymnals, Bibles, and tithe/offering envelopes are placed in the pew racks. They pick up the trash, and secure the doors until the next scheduled service. And they do it all with an attitude of praise.

Conclusion

With God guiding the members of the local Seventh-day Adventist churches in using the representative form of government, they will elect persons that possess the biblical qualifications needed to serve as deacons and deaconesses. As these officers follow the prescribed job description, and are empowered by the church to perform their multifaceted responsibilities of solving problems, nurturing the members, proclaiming the gospel, and serving as doorkeepers that work in the treasury, keep inventory of supplies, equipment, and sacred vessels, and open and secure the doors; the church will grow spiritually and numerically like the first century Christian church grew.

PART IV

The Work of the Deacon and Deaconess

Introduction

The office of deacon and deaconess provides an excellent opportunity for service within the church. The faithfulness of these dedicated officers can have a tremendous impact on the total church program in the following areas: the care and nurture of the membership, the comfort of the worshippers, the atmosphere of the services, and the care and appearance of the church property.[1]

Deacons are ordained to this service by the laying on of hands, according to Acts 6:5-6. The *Church Manual* states,

> A newly elected deacon cannot fill his office until he has been set apart by an ordained minister who holds current credentials from the conference/mission/field.
>
> The sacred rite of ordination should be simply performed in the presence of the church by an ordained minister, and may consist of a brief reference to the office of deacon, the qualities required of such a servant of the church, and the principle duties he will be authorized to perform for the church. After a short exhortation to faithfulness in service, the minister, assisted by an elder where appropriate, ordains the deacon by prayer and the laying on of hands. If he has been once ordained as deacon, and has maintained his membership, it is not necessary for him to be ordained again even though he has transferred to another church.[2]

The call to serve as a deacon is primarily a spiritual calling that requires spiritual qualifications very similar to those of the pastor and

---

[1]General Conference of Seventh-day Adventists, *Manual for Church Officers* (Washington, DC: Ministerial Assn., 1978), 83.

[2]General Conference of Seventh-day Adventists, *Church Manual*, 56.

elders. It is important that deacons be made aware of this concept before accepting the office. This will avoid role confusion as they seek to carry out their responsibilities. The *Manual for Church Officers* addresses the implications regarding the spiritual qualifications required of deacons. It states:

> This implies that much more is required of them than taking up the offering, maintaining the building and grounds, and occasionally distributing food to the poor. If a deacon, with the spiritual maturity demanded by the Scriptures for that office, is never called upon to reach out to higher horizons in service than this characteristic role, he is likely to become disillusioned and frustrated. This being so, it becomes important to understand the true concept of service involved in this office. Although the work involves the care of properties, the handling of monies, and other material or temporal matters, it is all for a spiritual purpose.[3]

The work of deaconesses is also a spiritual calling. Their maternal intuition equips them to comfort and encourage the sick and suffering. They are indeed angels of mercy to the sick.

Deaconesses are to "be grave, not slanderers, sober, faithful in all things" (1 Tim 3:11). The *Manual for Church Officers* gives this counsel:

> In personal appearance and dress, they are to be an example of modesty and decorum, as God's word enjoins. "In like manner also, that women adorn themselves in modest apparel" (chap. 2:9). Commenting on this scripture, Ellen White declares, "This forbids display in dress, gaudy colors, profuse ornamentation. Any device designed to attract attention to the wearer or to excite admiration, is excluded from the modest apparel which God's word enjoins." (*The Ministry of Healing*, p. 287).

The influence of godly deaconesses in a church can do much to permeate the entire congregation with the true spirit

---

[3]General Conference of Seventh-day Adventists, *Manual for Church Officers*, 83.

of love and service and exemplary living.[4]

It can be seen from this statement that the work of deaconesses is very important to the church. Based upon the action taken at the 59th General Conference session, June 24-July 3, 2010 in Atlanta, GA, deaconesses will be ordained along with the deacons as they begin their ministry. Part IV consists of the following chapters:

17   Serving During the Services of the Church

18   Holy Communion Services

19   The Ministry of Visitation

20   Deacons and Deaconesses as Physical Plant Managers

21   Organizing a Telephone Committee

Conclusion

---

[4]Ibid., 97.

Therefore, brethren, pick out from among you seven men of good repute, full of the Spirit and of wisdom, whom we may appoint to this duty. But we will devote ourselves to prayer and to the ministry of the word. And the word of God increased, and the number of the disciples multiplied in Jerusalem greatly.

Acts 6:3-4, 7 (RSV)

I commend to you our sister Phoebe, a deaconess of the church at Cenchreae, that you may receive her in whatever she may require from you, for she has been a helper of many and of myself as well.

Rom 16:1-2 (RSV)

CHAPTER 17

Serving During the Services of the Church

The duties of deacons and deaconesses are multifaceted. According to the qualifications required of them, they are multi-talented people.

The *Church Manual* lists the following duties for deacons and deaconesses: (1) assistance at services and meetings, (2) visitation of members, (3) preparation for baptismal services, (4) assistance at the Communion service, (5) care of the sick and the poor, and (6) care and maintenance of church property. Deaconesses are to assist in duties number 3, 4, and 5.[5]

Ushering

The instruction given that pertains to the duty of assistance at services and meetings is, "At church services, the deacons are usually responsible for welcoming members and visitors as they enter the church, and for assisting them, where necessary, to find seats. They also stand ready to cooperate with pastor and elders for the smooth functioning of the meetings conducted in the church."[6] To assign this duty to the deacons, and I propose to the deaconesses also, is in harmony with one of the responsibilities of the deaconesses during the first five centuries of the Christian church. I will again cite Riley, who gives this account, based upon the *Apostolic Constitution in Church Discipline, Doctrine, and Worship*: "During the first five Christian centuries, some of the help rendered by the deaconesses was to assist the presbyter in the baptism of women: greet the women parishioners, direct them to their seats, and maintain order among them."[7]

This is a perfect example of the role confusion and displacement

---

[5]General Conference of Seventh-day Adventist, *Church Manual*, 57-58.

[6]Ibid., 57.

[7]Riley, 1.

of deacons and deaconesses that was mentioned in chapter 5. Although it is historically documented and stated in the *Church Manual* since 1995 (maybe earlier) that deacons/deaconesses are to carry out this duty, ushers and greeters have been assigned to do it in the majority of the local Seventh-day Adventist churches. Therefore, the challenge for the Seventh-day Adventist church in the twenty-first century is to increase its awareness of the responsibilities of deacons and deaconesses, and to allow these officers to carry out their responsibilities. Although Naylor recognizes that in some churches persons other than deacons serve as ushers, he concludes, ". . . it is readily apparent that no one could serve more efficiently as an usher than a deacon."[8] Then he hastens to add, "No deacon should be satisfied, however, to be only an average usher."[9] If deacons serve as ushers, Naylor challenges them to strive to become the best ushers possible.

Since welcoming members and visitors as they enter the church and assisting them to find seats is the responsibility of deacons and deaconesses, it seems logical that these officers should oversee the ushering, or at least be involved in ushering in some way. However, it is also important to understand that there is to be no competition between deacons and deaconesses and the existing usher board, if there is one. With the skillful assistance of the pastor, these officers can work harmoniously together to accomplish this important ministry. Therefore, based upon the needs of each individual local church, I recommend the following job description taken from the Church Resources Consortium:

   Duties of the Usher

   1. Greet worshippers, making every attempt to help them feel welcome and at ease.
   2. Escort members and guests to their seats.
   3. Distribute materials related to the service/meeting such as bulletins, hymnals, handouts, etc.

---

[8]Naylor, 84.

[9]Ibid.

4. Receive certain offerings, delivering them properly to the treasury department of the church.
5. Maintain an alertness for any emergency that may arise, relieving the need or contacting the person(s) needed to provide the proper assistance.
6. Direct individuals out of the service/meeting in an orderly fashion (in most instances row by row), leaving the auditorium or room ready for the next service or meeting.[10]

I also recommend some additional services for the deacons and deaconesses/ushers to consider as they carry out their usher ministry. I recommend that they view the members and visitors who sit in the pews that they monitor as their parish. They should get to know those individuals, call them during the week to pray with them, call them when they are absent from church, send them cards on special occasions, and offer assistance to those needing help caring for their children. Seek God's guidance in developing this into a small group ministry where Bible studies and social events can be held in their homes. This could also develop into outreach ministries in their neighborhoods.

Rendering assistance at services and meetings requires that the deacons and deaconesses become more involved in all of the services of the church, such as Sabbath School, Divine Worship, Adventist Youth Society (AYS), Mid-Week Prayer Meeting, Funerals, Baptisms, and Holy Communion.

Sabbath School

Deacons and deaconesses should make every effort to be present at Sabbath School. They should study their lessons carefully, and be prepared to teach a Sabbath school class if needed.

In fact, since their calling is a spiritual calling and they are

---

[10]Church Resources Consortium, North American Division of Seventh-day Adventist Church, "Usher Ministry Description," *Responsibilities in the Local Church*, http://www.plusline.org/article .php?id=320 (accessed November 22, 2010).

equipped to teach the Work of God, it would be most appropriate for the Sabbath school council to consider selecting some of these officers to serve as Sabbath school teachers.

The assigned deacon(s) should arrive at least an hour before Sabbath school begins to open the doors and make sure that the church is properly heated or cooled for service. The other deacons and deaconesses should arrive at least thirty minutes before Sabbath school begins so they can help greet the worshipers as they arrive, and help maintain reverence.

If the ushers need their assistance, the deacons and deaconesses should help them distribute the church bulletins, place the offering envelopes and hymnals in the racks of the pews, escort visitors to the adult division or pastor's class, escort visitors with children to the lower division to leave their children, then escort them back to the adult division or pastor's class.

Divine Worship Services

During the Divine Worship Service, the deacons play an important role in the collection of tithes and offerings. This function should be conducted in a carefully organized and graceful manner. The head deacon is to develop a quarterly duty roster which includes a schedule for the deacons who are to participate in this part of the service. When an assigned deacon is unable to fulfill his responsibility, he should inform the head deacon and arrange to have a substitute. The number of deacons involved in this process will be determined by the size of the congregation and the layout of the sanctuary. "For the small churches, it may seem to be a simple task. Unfortunately, however, it is often in the small churches that order, system, and finesse are most lacking."[11] The deacons should dress uniformly when serving in this capacity. They should wear black or navy suits, black shoes, white shirts, and black ties (or other agreed upon ties). It is important that the deacons place the offering plates at the altar before the service starts.

The procedure used for collecting tithes and offerings will vary

---

[11]General Conference of Seventh-day Adventists, *Manual for Church Officers*, 87.

from church to church, however, there are some basic similarities. The following is an example.

When the elder calls for the tithes and offerings, the deacons seated in the front will rise from their seats and walk together and stand in front of the pulpit. If they are positioned in various areas of the sanctuary prior to the offering, they will still come forward together in a uniform manner. The elder will pause to allow them to pick up the offering plates and distribute them among themselves. Then he will say a brief prayer. The deacons should work in pairs. They will march abreast to their designated areas and pass the plate down the pews. They should handle the offering plates with care, holding them with both hands.

When the offering has been received, the deacons march to the rear of the church and wait until the elder asks the congregation to stand. They will then march to the front of the pulpit, keeping abreast by twos, as the elder concludes the reading of Malachi 3:8-10. After the elder offers the prayer of dedication and the congregation sings the hymn of response, the deacons who are assigned to take the offering plates to the treasury room, do so at this time. The other deacons march to their seats in an orderly manner.

> The deacons should count the cash in the offerings, then list the amount on a slip of paper over the signature of the head deacon and turn it over to the church treasurer. The treasurer will give a receipt to the deacon for the cash. Enough deacons should be used for this task so that it will be done rapidly. This is a safeguard to the treasurer. In some churches one or more of the deacons takes the offering directly to the bank. Often the church has a safe in the building in which to keep money. The treasurer or deacon should not keep the money in his home.[12]

In large churches, it may be necessary that the deacons rehearse this process of collecting tithes and offering at least once a quarter in order to minimize mistakes.

Deaconesses should dress uniformly when serving during the Divine Worship Service. They should dress in white outfits, especially

---

[12]Ibid.

during the spring and summer months. Some deaconess boards wear black or navy suits in the fall and winter.

At least one deaconess should be assigned to sit in the nursing room to assist parents with babies and toddlers as needed. She should also assist the usher that is assigned to this room to maintain reverence and order.

The deaconesses that are seated on the front pew of the sanctuary should assist the person telling the children's story during the Children Chapel to keep the children quiet and orderly. They should pay close attention to special needs that may arise, such as, a child with a runny nose, an upset stomach, a coughing or crying spell, spilled milk, etc.

Deaconesses should seek to maintain reverence in the areas where they are seated. They should also feel free to go to where a disturbance is in order to resolve it, or get the attention of an usher or deacon so that he/she will go and resolve it. It is important to be discreet and tactful when dealing with disturbances. It is also important to pray for wisdom before deciding to act. Judge whether or not addressing a particular disturbance will create a greater problem than the present one.

Deaconesses are to make sure that the water pitcher and glasses behind the pulpit are clean. The water should be fresh and room temperature. Cold water will damage the speaker's vocal cords. If the pitcher does not have a lid, keep it covered with a napkin, and turn the glasses upside down on a napkin. Bottle water can be used instead of tap water. This would alleviate the need for a pitcher. The pastor or speaker may request some juice in addition to water; therefore, it would be a good idea to keep some on hand.

The head deaconess should make a duty roster and rotate the deaconesses to carry out these assignments. When the Divine Worship Service is over, the deaconesses, deacons, and ushers should see to it that the hymnals and Bibles are put back in the pew racks correctly, paper and trash are picked up off of the floor and pews, items left are taken to the lost and found area, and the church is securely locked.

Adventist Youth Society (AYS)

The deacons' and deaconesses' presence at AYS speaks volumes to the youth of the church. It indicates that they have an interest in the development of the youth. By attending these meetings, the deacons and deaconesses have an opportunity to establish rapport with the youth.

AYS can serve as a practicum for the junior deacons and deaconesses of the church. During these meetings, they can take the lead in carrying out the responsibilities that they have been instructed in and have observed and assisted the adult deacons and deaconesses do during the Divine Worship Services.

Although it is not necessary for the junior deacons to dress in uniform at AYS, they should, however, dress appropriately. By this I mean they should not dress faddishly, their clothing should fit them properly, and their hair appropriately cut and styled. They are to recognize that they are the spiritual leaders among the youth and should seek to set a godly example for them.

Some of the duties that the junior deacons and deaconesses would carry out at AYS are: collect the offering, maintain reverence, and see to it that the hymnals and Bibles are put back in the pew racks correctly, and that all paper and trash are picked up off of the floor and pews.

It is important that the head deacon and head deaconess schedule at least one of their workers to be present to give support to their junior counterparts, and address any emergency that may arise.

Mid-Week Prayer Meetings

Deacons and deaconesses should make every effort to attend mid-week prayer meetings. Their presence is just as important as that of the pastor and elders. They too are spiritual leaders of the church, and are to set an example for the membership.

The pastor and first elder should schedule them to participate on the program. They may be scheduled to lead the song service, take prayer requests and testimonies, or present a message from time to time.

But even when they are not carrying out these responsibilities, the deacons should collect the offering, make sure that the church is properly heated or cooled, maintain reverence, and be supportive of the pastor or elders who are leading out in the service.

The head deacon and head deaconess should assign deacons and deaconesses to each of the services of the church. Their presence will be a constant reminder to the membership that they are spiritual leaders.

It is important that when the deacons and deaconesses attend the mid-week prayer meeting that they dress appropriately. The deacons should wear coats and ties. The deaconesses should wear dresses, suits, or skirts and blouses. The way one dresses has a great deal to do with the respect he or she receives. The misconception that deacons are church janitors is only strengthened when they come to church in work clothes. Some members may find it difficult to give due respect to deacons and deaconesses that enter the Sanctuary dressed inappropriately. Also visitors should be able to identify the leaders of the church by their dress. At least, their appropriate dress should be an indicator. Deacons might consider keeping a set of work clothes in their car or at the church for emergency situations.

Funerals

The love of the church for its members and their families is severely tested when death occurs. The deacons and deaconesses can be a tremendous source of comfort during this time. The following are some basic duties to be performed by them:

1. Unless otherwise assigned, the head deaconess has the responsibility to send flowers from the church to the family of the deceased members

2. The deaconesses will plan food for the bereaved family on the day of the funeral. Determine the number of relatives expected, so that the needs will be met. Also, plan the most appropriate time to deliver the food. During these periods of grief, both deacons and deaconesses should visit the family as representatives of the church.[13]

3. The deacons are to assist the deaconesses with setting up for the meal, if the family is to be served at the church, or some other facility.

4. The deaconesses are to serve as flower bearers and the

_____

[13]Ibid., 100.

deacons are to serve as pall bearers if needed.

FUNERAL COMMITTEE

In addition to performing these basic duties, the deacons and deaconesses should constantly seek ways to enhance their ministry to the bereaved. It is important that they become more involved with the family at a personal level, by providing support and consultation for them. One of the ways that this can be accomplished is by establishing a Funeral Committee. This committee should consist of deacons, deaconesses, and other interested church members. In order for this committee to provide optimum service, its members must be knowledgeable of the resources and service providers in the community. It is important that they have a good relationship with these providers, and be able to network with them.

When the coordinator of this committee is made aware of a death, he/she should contact the pastor and the leaders of the following departments: hospitality, deacons, deaconesses, ushers, audio-visual, music, and nursery. The coordinator will communicate information to these department leaders about the status of the family's decisions concerning the time, date, and place of the funeral.

Based upon the needs of the family, the Funeral Committee will provide the following services:

1. A "Things To Do" list to prepare for a funeral.
2. A list of hotels for out-of-town relatives/guests
3. A list of church members who are willing to house out-of-town relatives/guests
4. Pick up out-of-town relatives from airport and other public transportation facilities. Take them back when they are ready to leave.

On the day of the funeral, the Funeral Committee coordinator should designate a few committee members to arrive one hour prior to the viewing, to accomplish the following:

1. Set up a room in which the family will meet prior to the service. Provide water, juice, cups, and tissues.
2. Reserve pews in the sanctuary for the family and program

participants. Place boxes of tissues in the pews where the family will be seated

3. Locate all program participates and introduce them to the officiating minister
4. See that program participants have bulletins
5. Be available to serve as a messenger for the minister and the family
6. Arrange for the minister to pray with and share information with the family, in the gathering room, prior to the processional
7. See that all arrangements for the meal have been made
8. See that a nurse and a physician are present to handle any emergency

In carrying out the above services, be careful to follow trends in your locale and cooperate fully with the funeral directors and ministers.

The Funeral Committee Coordinator should assign at least two committee members to do follow-up with the family. The follow-up period may vary from two months to twelve months, depending upon the need. It is extremely important to make contact with the family during holidays, wedding anniversary date, birthday, and anniversary date of death. The contacts should be in the form of personal visits, telephone calls, and/or cards.[14]

An ideal booklet to use in assisting families to plan funerals is *Funeral Planning Made Simple*, 4th ed. by R. Steven Norman, III. GESS Books International, 1995.

Baptismal Services

The third duty listed in the *Church Manual* for deacons and deaconesses is preparing for and assisting at baptismal services.

At this ceremony the deacons should make the necessary preparation and assist the male candidates into and out of the

---

[14]Portions of this section were submitted by Teresa Banks, Funeral Committee of the Breath of Life Seventh-day Adventist Church, Fort Washington, MD, 1999.

water. The deaconesses should assist all female candidates. Care should be exercised to see that proper attire is provided for the candidates. Robes of suitable heavy material are preferable. If such are not available, the candidates should dress in such a manner that they will be modestly attired. The baptismal ceremony should be followed by extending the right hand of fellowship and the giving of a few words of welcome by the pastor or elder in behalf of the entire church.[15]

There are three basic areas of concern for a person who has decided to be baptized. These areas are the mode, the prerequisites, and the age.

The mode of baptism is derived from the meaning of the word. The Greek word βαπτίζω comes from βάπτω which means to dip, to immerse.[16] Two biblical examples of baptism by immersion are found in Mark 1:9-10 and Acts 8:38-39.

The prerequisites for baptism are having faith in Jesus, repentance from sins, a conversion experience, and being properly taught all that Jesus has commanded us to do (Mark 16:15-16; Acts 2:37-38; 3:19; Matt 28:18-20).

The age of the person being baptized is only an issue if the person is an infant or a young child. Infants and young children do not meet the prerequisites for baptism. They are not capable of understanding this biblical teaching. Therefore, persons must be of an age that they can make responsible decisions about their own faith.

The following are some additional instructions for the deacons and deaconesses at the baptism service:

1. The deacons should clean and fill the baptistry in plenty of time before the service so that the water level and temperature are appropriate.
2. The head deaconess should make sure that enough robes (proper sizes), bath towels, wash cloths, bathing caps, and

---

[15]General Conference of Seventh-day Adventists, *Church Manual*, 35.

[16]Moulton, s.v. "βαπτίζω."

socks are on hand before the day of the service. White is an appropriate color for all of these items. Items should be stored in a secure place close to the dressing rooms.

3. The head deacon and head deaconess should have extra clothing and robes on hand for persons who may decide to participate at the last moment. The head deaconess should also have some nail polish remover and wipes handy.

4. The head deacon and head deaconess should privately call the pastor's attention to candidates who may be wearing colorful cosmetics and jewelry, before the service begins.

5. The head deacon and head deaconess should obtain from the pastor instructions regarding the order in which the candidates are to enter the baptistry. They should have each candidate place his/her name, address, telephone number, date of birth, and date of baptism on a 3x5 card before the service begins. All cards are given to the pastor.

6. The head deacon assigns other deacons to assist male candidates change clothes, and to enter and exit the baptistry. The head deaconess does likewise regarding the female candidates.

7. If the baptism follows the sermon during Sabbath service, the deacons and deaconesses are to assist the candidates to get dressed immediately after Sabbath school. They sit with the candidates on the front rows during worship service, making sure that they are comfortable. After the pastor reads the baptismal vows to the candidates, the deacons and deaconesses escort them to the baptistry.

8. The deaconesses wrap the baptized female candidates with a sheet as they ascend the steps of the baptistry, and escort them back to the dressing room. A deaconess is to be stationed outside of the dressing room door, to secure the privacy of the candidates.

9. After the baptism, the candidates dress and are escorted back to the Sanctuary to receive the right hand of fellowship.

10. Upon completion of the service, the deacons and deaconesses gather the wet items that belong to the church, so that they can be laundered and properly stored until needed again.

11. The deacons are responsible for draining the baptistry. However, if the water is to remain for another baptism in the

near future, chlorine should be placed in the water.

12. After sunset, a thorough cleaning of the dressing rooms and areas leading to the baptistry should be done by the deacons and deaconesses.

Other important items for the deacons and deaconesses to consider are the robes should be made from a material that cannot be seen through and heavy enough to stay down in the water. The preferred colors are white or black. Make sure that the dressing rooms have adequate space and are heated and attractive. Finally, check the baptistry heater periodically and keep it in operating condition.

CHAPTER 18

Holy Communion Services

The fourth duty listed in the *Church Manual* for deacons and deaconesses is arranging for and assisting at the Communion services.

> At the celebration of the ordinance of foot-washing, the deacons or deaconesses provide everything that is needed for the service, such as: towels, basins, water (at a comfortable temperature as the occasion may require), buckets, et cetera. After the service they should see that the vessels and linen used are washed and returned to their proper place.
>
> Following the Lord's Supper, great care should be exercised in disposing of any bread or wine left over after all have partaken of these emblems. Any remaining wine that was blessed is to be respectfully poured out. Any remaining bread that was blessed should be buried, burned, or respectfully disposed of in another appropriate manner but in no event returned to common usage.
>
> The deaconesses make arrangements for the communion table, including: preparing the bread and wine, arranging the ordinance table, pouring the wine, placing the plates of unleavened bread, and covering the table with the linen provided for that purpose. All these matters should be cared for before the service begins.[17]

Foot-Washing

According to John 13:1-10, the ordinance of foot-washing is a miniature baptism. Whereas baptism represents the washing away of our sinful past, foot-washing represents the washing away of our present faults, misunderstandings, and differences that we have with others. The *Minister's Manual* states,

---

[17]General Conference of Seventh-day Adventists, *Church Manual*, 57-58.

Foot washing is a time for making wrongs right, for reaching out to those with whom you have differed, and this should be emphasized. This kind of alienation takes place quite often between husband and wife or between parents and teenage children. Communion day can become a beautiful time for uniting families.[18]

The spiritual preparation for Holy Communion should begin at least one week before the service. The pastor, elders, deacons, and deaconesses should:

1. Renew their personal relationship with God through prayer and seeking forgiveness.
2. Review the Scriptures and Spirit of Prophecy readings that deal with the Lord's Supper (Matt 26:17-30; Mark 14:12-26; Luke 22:7-39; John 13:1-17; 1 Cor 10; 11:17-34; *The Desire of Ages* 642-787).
3. Seek forgiveness from persons they may have offended.
4. Forgive those who have offended them—assuring them that they have been forgiven.
5. Pastor or elder should prepare a Spirit-filled sermon that is brief and relevant for the occasion.

The following areas should be considered, as relating to the physical preparations and service:

1. All preparations should be done ahead of time, preferably before the Sabbath. Hand wipes or soap and water should be available to wash hands after foot-washing.
2. "Deacons and deaconesses should participate in the foot-washing service, but preferably they should have done it earlier, perhaps when setting up the equipment."[19] This will prevent delaying the Lord's Supper.
3. The head deacon will lead the men and the head deaconess

---

[18]General Conference of Seventh-day Adventists, *Minister's Manual* (Silver Spring, MD: Ministerial Assn., 1992), 214.

[19]Ibid., 215.

will lead the women. They will see that everyone has been served; and lead out in singing, testimonies, and prayer. Keep the testimonies brief so as many as desire might participate.

4. The deacons and deaconesses should be very tactful with the parents of children who do not understand the meaning of the service. If a parent insists that his/her child understands the meaning of the service, allow the child to participate under the parent's supervision. The same rule applies in the child's participation in the ordinance of the Lord's Supper.

5. The head deacon and head deaconess are to remind the people of any special seating arrangements to take place in the sanctuary before they return to the sanctuary for the Lord's Supper. If the congregation is small, it is recommended that the people sit every other pew, beginning with the third pew from the front (if deacons and deaconesses will be seated on the front pews). If the congregation is too large for this arrangement, the people should leave enough space at both ends of the pews so that the deacons serving from both ends can reach and serve those seated in the center of the pews. The other option is to have the people leave enough space at the end of the pews closest to the center aisle(s) so that the deacons serving from the center aisle can reach and serve everyone seated in the center of the pews (see diagrams at end of chapter).

The Lord's Supper

Reverence and graceful harmonious movements are of the utmost importance in this service. Nothing less is acceptable. Therefore, it is a must that the pastor, elders, deacons, and deaconesses have a rehearsal prior to this undertaking. It is suggested that the rehearsal occurs the night prior to the service. Only those who attend the rehearsal should play a leading role in the service. The service is not a time to rehearse. The service is a time for graceful harmonious movements.

Churches with a Small Membership

1. The Participants

The pastor should utilize as many elders, deacons, and deaconesses as possible to lead out without having the service appear too cumbersome. The number used will depend upon the size of the congregation, the number of emblem trays, and the number of officers that attended the rehearsal. The maximum number of participants behind the table should be four: the pastor, first elder, and two other elders. For this illustration, the following officers are the leading participants: the pastor, first elder, two other elders, four deacons, and four deaconesses.

2.   The Processional

The congregation is seated as instructed by the deacons and deaconess. All of the officers line up in the foyer (or other designated area). This includes even those who did not attend the rehearsal. Everyone is a part of the processional if they are properly dressed: deacons—black suit, white shirt, white gloves, and white tie (or some other agreed upon tie); deaconesses—white dress, white gloves and white cap (some deaconess boards wear black or navy suits, especially in the winter); pastor and elders—black suit, white shirt, white tie (or some other agreed upon tie).

The processional takes place down the center aisle. Each deaconess marches at the right side of a deacon (matching heights as nearly as possible). It is important that a deacon and a deaconess who attended the rehearsal lead the way. The two deaconesses assigned to unveil the table will be the last deaconesses in the line. In front of them will be the two deaconesses assigned to veil the table. The pastor and elders line up behind the deacons and deaconesses. The first elder will be at the pastor's right side. The other two elders that will participate behind the table will pair off behind them.

The deacons, deaconesses, pastor and elders march down the center aisle, starting out on their left foot. The deaconesses will march to the right front pew, and the deacons will march to the left front pew. The deacon and deaconess leading the procession will go far enough down the pew so that the last deacon and deaconess marching in will be positioned nearest the center aisle.

The pastor marches behind the table around the left side, while the first elder marches to the right. The next two elders will follow the pastor and the first elder behind the table.

All of the officers are now standing in place facing the front. They remain standing until the pastor signals them, by nodding his head, to be seated. The pastor and the three elders behind the table will remain standing throughout the service (diagram at end of chapter).

3. The Procedure

The congregation remains seated, and the officers remain standing, while a hymn of meditation is sung. After the first stanza is completed, the pastor signals, by nodding his head, for the two deaconesses assigned to unveil the table to come forth. The singing continues while the table is unveiled (for details, see section on "Unveiling and Veiling the Table"). The two deaconesses return to their front pew positions, the pastor nods and all of the officers are seated (except the pastor and elders behind the table). At this time, the singing ceases, and the suggested order of service may be followed, beginning at Holy Scripture Read (see page 127).

Churches with a Medium or Large Membership

1. The Participants

The same principle used to determine the number of participants for a church with a small membership is used for a medium and large church membership. The number of leading participants will depend upon the number of emblem trays on hand and the number of officers that attended the rehearsal.

2. The Processional

The congregation is seated as instructed by the deacons and deaconesses—either leaving enough space at both ends of the pews, or at the end of the pews closest to the center aisle.

All of the officers line up in the foyer (or other designated area). This includes even those who did not attend the rehearsal. Everyone is a part of the processional, provided they are in uniform, as previously described.

For this illustration, there are twelve elders, twelve deacons, twelve deaconesses, the first elder, and the pastor. The processional takes place down the two center aisles in front of the platform. The deacons pair off in twos at the left center aisle. The pastor will line up behind them, and six of the elders will pair off and line up behind him. The deaconesses will line up at the right center aisle. The two deaconesses assigned to unveil the table and the two assigned to veil the table should be paired-off and positioned in line so that they will be seated closest to the table. The rest of the deaconesses will line up by twos accordingly. The first elder will line up behind the deaconesses, and the other six elders will pair off and line up behind him. Everyone should select a person of similar height to pair off with. It is important that the deacons and deaconesses that attended the rehearsal be at the front of the processional.

The deacons, deaconesses, elders, and pastor march down their respective aisles starting out on their left foot. Based upon eight persons occupying a pew, upon reaching the front pews, the two deaconesses assigned to veil the table will march to the center of the front center pew, followed by the two deaconesses assigned to unveil the table. The remaining eight deaconesses will march to the front right pew. The first four deacons will march to the front center pew to join the four deaconesses that will unveil and veil the table. The remaining eight deacons will march to the front left pew. The pastor will march behind the table from the left side, followed by six elders. The first elder will march behind the table from the right side, followed by six elders. The six elders to the right of the pastor will stand abreast, slightly behind the pastor, and the six elders to the left of the first elder are positioned the same. The pastor and elders will stand facing the congregation.

The deacons and deaconesses are standing in place facing the table. They remain standing until the pastor signals them, by nodding his head, to be seated. The pastor and elders behind the table will remain standing throughout the service (diagram at end of chapter).

3.   The Procedure

The procedure is the same as for small churches.

THE LORD'S SUPPER
(Order of Service)

Introit	Pianist/Organist
Processional	Officers

****

Hymn of Meditation 163 "At the Cross"	Congregation
Holy Table Unveiled	Deaconesses
Holy Scripture Read I Cor. 11:23-24	Pastor
Holy Bread Blessed	Elder
Holy Washing (hand washing)	Pastor & 1st Elder
Holy Bread Broken	Pastor & 1st Elder
Holy Bread Served	Deacons
Hymn of Meditation 158 "Were You There?"	Congregation

****

Holy Scripture Read I Cor. 11:25-26	Pastor
Holy Wine Blessed	Elder
Holy Wine Served	Deacons
Hymn of Meditation 336 "There is A Fountain"	Congregation
Holy Glasses Retrieved	Deacons

****

Holy Table Veiled	Deaconesses
Testimonies (small groups, if not done during service)	Congregation
Hymn of Discipleship 598 "Watch Ye Saints"	Congregation
Benediction	Pastor
Recessional	Officers
	Congregation

****

Benevolent Offering (Collected at the door)	Deacons

POINTS TO REMEMBER

1. The head deacon and head deaconess should assign the deacons and deaconesses who will be the leading participants for each Holy Communion service throughout the year. These assignments should be made well in advance of the services so that these officers will plan to attend the rehearsals.
2. Inspect all equipment the week before the service.
3. The deaconesses assigned to unveil and veil the table are the only persons to assist in this process. If a mistake is made, let them handle it. The pastor will use his discretion in offering his assistance, or requesting the assistance of others. It would be safe to apply this principle to every situation. Let the officer(s) assigned to do a task do it. If anything unexpected happens during the service, before reacting, follow the pastor's lead.
4. The pastor should be the only one to arrange/rearrange the trays on the table. If he needs assistance, he will signal. Therefore, it is important to pay close attention to his movements and facial expressions. If he has to speak, he will speak in a whisper. So please stay alert.
5. It is especially important that the deacons, deaconesses, and elders stay focused on the service. Do not get so caught-up in singing, talking, reading the bulletin, etc., that you fail to observe the pastor's signals. Do not bring anything that may cause a distraction, such as: pocketbooks, Bibles, cell phones, pagers, children, bulletins, tape recorders, coats, etc. Keep your eyes on the pastor.
6. The pastor and the first elder will pass and retrieve the bread and wine trays to and from the elders behind the table. These elders will pass and retrieve the trays to and from the deacons. The trays should be held close to the front of the body at waist level, with both hands, and thumbs on top.
7. When the deacons serve the bread and wine to the congregation (and when they retrieve the cups), they should begin at the center of the pews and work toward the ends.
8. After the deacons have served the congregation, they will line-up in twos at the rear of the center aisle(s) facing the table, just as they were for the processional. The pastor will check to see if everyone has been served by asking, "Has anyone been

overlooked?" If someone raises his/her hand, the deacon nearest to him/her will assist. This is done during the serving of the bread and wine, and when retrieving the glasses.

9. When everyone has been served, the pastor will nod his head and the deacons will march to the table. The pastor nods and each deacon gives his tray to the elder that he received it from. The pastor nods and the deacons march to their seats.

10. Once the deacons are seated, the pastor nods and the elders go and serve the deacons and deaconesses. Another option is that the pastor and first elder serve the deacons, deaconesses, and elders.

11. If the former is used, upon returning to their positions behind the table, the elders give their trays to the pastor and first elder. The pastor and first elder will stack the trays on the table, but will use the last tray they receive to serve the elders. The first elder will place his tray on the table and the pastor will serve him. The first elder will then take the tray from the pastor's hand and serve him. The pastor retrieves the tray, places it on the table, and says to the congregation, "Let us eat/drink together."

12. Repeat numbers 6-11 when serving the wine and retrieving the glasses. If disposable glasses are used, let the people keep them for a memento.

13. To keep from prolonging the service, members are asked to share their testimonies with each other after the table has been veiled. They may also do it while the bread and wine are being served. If the latter is done, have an adequate number of persons with microphones to take to the people.

14. After the benediction, the pastor reminds the congregation to give a special offering to the benevolent fund on their way out. A deacon or usher stands at the door with an offering plate to receive the offerings.

15. At the recessional, the deacons and deaconesses will pair off and march out, in the reverse order of the processional. The elders and pastor will pair off and join in (diagram at end of chapter). The ushers direct the recession of the congregation.

16. After the deaconesses have prepared the Holy Communion Kits for the sick and shut-ins, the un-used blessed bread and wine are gathered for proper disposal. The bread is to be burned or buried. The wine is to be poured on the ground. The deaconesses clear

the table and see to it that the linen cloths and trays are properly cared for. The deacons are responsible for re-positioning the table.

17. If a briefer service is desired, see *Church Manual*, p. 97-98, or *Minister's Manual*, p. 216.

The Lord's Supper for the Sick and Shut-ins

If there are members confined at home or hospital, a special service may be conducted for them. The head deacon is responsible for contacting the men, and the head deaconess should contact the women a week prior to Holy Communion. Contact them again the day before as a reminder. This will give them time to prepare or to indicate that they choose not to participate.

Foot washing is generally omitted in the home or the hospital. Usually the sick are not physically able to participate. When the head deacon and head deaconess call the sick members, they may ask them if they desire to have their feet washed. The deacons and deaconesses should carry towels and basins with them for those who choose to participate. The deacons will assist the men, and the deaconesses will assist the women. The pastor or elder, and deacons will step out while the deaconesses wash the women's feet.

When possible, a team consisting of the pastor or an ordained elder, a deacon, and a deaconess should provide Holy Communion for the sick and shut-in. However, it is not necessary for the team to partake in the foot washing and the emblems, since they participated at church.

After exchanging greetings and inquiring about the patient's health, the suggested format is followed, with the pastor or elder officiating, and the deacon and deaconess assisting.

A. A "brief" summary of the sermon
B. Prayer
C. Open the portable Holy Communion kit and prepare emblems
D. Scripture reading (I Cor. 11:23, 24)
E. Bless the bread
F. Serve the bread
G. Scripture reading (I Cor. 11:25, 26)

H. Bless the wine
I. Serve the wine
J. Sing a hymn
K. Testimonies
L. Benediction

Note: This same format can be used when giving Holy Communion to incarcerated members.

Proper Care of Holy Communion Vessels and Foot-Washing Equipment

1. All of the vessels and equipment used in the Lord's Supper and foot-washing are sacred. They should be treated as such.
2. The deaconesses are responsible for removing the linen cloths and trays from the table immediately after the service. They are to store them in a secure area, such as a storage cabinet, chest, or closet, until after sunset (if the service was on the Sabbath).
3. After sunset, the deaconesses should wash the trays, wrap them in plastic, and replace them in their secure area. The linen cloths, napkins, and towels should be laundered and properly stored until the next Holy Communion.
4. The deacons and deaconesses are responsible for disposing of the water, stacking basins and buckets, and bagging used towels immediately after foot washing. These items are to be secured until after sunset.
5. After sunset, the deacons are responsible for rearranging the chairs, and cleaning up the rooms used for foot-washing. They are to disinfect the basins and buckets, and store them in a secure area, such as a cabinet, chest, or closet, until the next foot-washing service. They should give the towels to the deaconesses to be washed and stored.

Unveiling and Veiling the Table

The unveiling and veiling of the table are very important aspects of the Holy Communion service. The unveiling sets the tone of the service and the veiling seals it. It is an awesome sight to behold the two deaconesses, as they skillfully move with precision.

UNVEILING THE TABLE

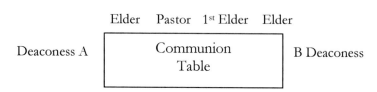

1.   Two deaconesses, (A & B), walk toward their designated end of the table. When they are approximately two feet from the table, they turn and face each other. Simultaneously, both of them will take two steps sideways toward the table, which will place them at the center of the ends of the table.

2.   Both of them will stoop, take hold of the corners of the linen cloth, and raise the cloth high enough to clear the vessels. While holding the cloth in the raised position, they will take two steps sideways toward the front of the table.

3.   The cloth is held at breast level, and stretched to keep it from drooping. A and B will bring the corner of the cloth in the hand that is closest to the table and place it in the hand that is closest to the congregation. A and B will reach down with the hand closest to the table and raise the folded corner of the cloth, and place it in the hand closest to the congregation. Then A and B will reach down again to take hold of the folded corner in the hand closest to the table, and raise it even with the other corner.

4.   A will walk toward B and place the corners of the cloth in her hands ½ inch below the top edge. A will stoop and raise the folded edge of the cloth and place it in B's hand ½ inch below the previous edge. A will repeat this step again and place the folded edge in B's hand ½ inch below the previous edge (layering the edges of the cloth ½ inch makes it easier to separate when veiling).

5.   B will either place the cloth on a designated small table near the front, or place it across her arm and take it to her seat.

6.   Both A and B will walk side by side to their seats.

VEILING THE TABLE

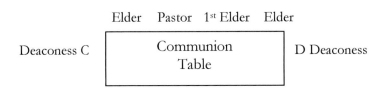

1. While Deaconesses C and D walk side by side toward the table, D retrieves the cloth from B or from the designated small table, making sure that the layered edges are facing away from her. Both C and D stand approximately two feet in front of the table, at the center, facing each other. C is on the left, and D is on the right.
2. D holds the cloth at breast level and C gracefully separates it one layer at a time, bringing each layer down. When there is only one layer left, C takes it by the two corners and begins to step backward, while D continues to hold the other two corners and steps backward also until the cloth is stretched.
3. Both C and D raise the corner of the cloth that is in the hand closest to the congregation, and lower the corner that is in the hand closest to the table simultaneously. With the hand closest to the table, C and D bring the fold down. With the hand closest to the table, both of them take hold of the corner closest to the table, and separate the corners by spreading their arms open simultaneously.
4. Holding the stretched cloth at breast level, C and D take two steps sideways toward the table, which will place them at the center of the ends of the table. They will gracefully lay the cloth over the table evenly. Do not allow the corners of the cloth to fall down, but stoop slightly while bringing the corners down.
5. Still facing each other and standing erectly, C and D will take two steps sideways toward the front of the table. D will do an about-face and pause until C walks up beside her. Then the both of them will walk to their seats and sit down.[20]

---

[20]Portions of this section were submitted by Eva Muwwakkil, former head deaconess of the Harvest Seventh-day Adventist Church, Harvest, AL, 1999.

Recipes for Communion Bread
and Unfermented Wine

COMMUNION BREAD

1 cup fine-ground flour (preferably whole grain)
¼ teaspoon salt
2 tablespoons cold water
¼ cup olive or vegetable oil

Method: Sift flour and salt together. Pour the water into the oil, but do not stir. Add this to the dry ingredients and mix with a fork until all the flour is dampened. Roll out between two sheets of waxed paper to the thickness of thick pie pastry [piecrust]. Place on an un-greased, floured baking sheet, and mark off with a sharp knife into bite-size squares, being careful to prick each square to prevent blistering. Bake at 450 degrees Fahrenheit for 10-15 minutes. Watch carefully during the last five minutes to prevent burning. Serves 50 persons.

ALTERNATE RECIPE FOR COMMUNION BREAD

1 cup fine-ground flour (preferably whole grain)
¼ teaspoon salt
3 tablespoons pure vegetable oil
4 ½ tablespoons cold water

Method: Put oil in bowl and add salt. Slowly add water, beating constantly with a fork until the ingredients make a thick, white emulsion. Quickly add the flour and mix lightly into a dough. Turn out on a floured board. Fold over and over and pound with a wooden mallet or potato masher until elastic (five or six minutes). Roll to the thickness of piecrust, place on an oiled baking sheet, and mark with a knife into bite-sized squares. Bake at 400 degrees Fahrenheit. Brown only slightly, as browning gives a strong flavor.

[Most of the bread should be broken by the deaconesses before it is placed on the table. However, leave a few pieces unbroken for the pastor and elders to break.]

UNFERMENTED WINE

Secure good grapes, strip them from the stem, and stew them in an enameled saucepan until they come to the boiling point. Strain through a course cloth, then boil for 15 minutes. Just before the juice boils, skim off the scum that rises. When the juice is at the boiling point, pour into strong bottles that have been sterilized and kept warm so they will receive the hot juice without breaking. Fill to within one-half inch of the cork, and cork immediately. Cut off the cork close to the bottle, and seal with sealing wax. Set aside in a dark place, and do not move the bottles unnecessarily.[21]

The Lords' Supper Seating Diagrams

Churches with a Small Membership

---

[21]General Conference of Seventh-day Adventists, *Minister's Manual*, 218.

Churches with a Medium or Large Membership

```
┌─────────────────────────────┐
│         Communion           │
│           Table             │
└─────────────────────────────┘
```

O O O O	O O O O	O O O O
O O O O	O O O O	O O O O
O O O O	O O O O	O O O O
O O O O	O O O O	O O O O
O O O O	O O O O	O O O O
O O O O	O O O O	O O O O
O O O O	O O O O	O O O O
O O O O	O O O O	O O O O

```
┌─────────────────────────────┐
│         Communion           │
│           Table             │
└─────────────────────────────┘
```

O O O O O	O O O O	O O O O O
O O O O O	O O O O	O O O O O
O O O O O	O O O O	O O O O O
O O O O O	O O O O	O O O O O
O O O O O	O O O O	O O O O O
O O O O O	O O O O	O O O O O
O O O O O	O O O O	O O O O O
O O O O O	O O O O	O O O O O

The Lord's Supper Processional Diagrams

Churches with a Small Membership

E   P   1ST E   E

```
┌─────────────────────────────┐
│        Communion            │
│          Table              │
└─────────────────────────────┘
```

4 3 2 1		A B C D

O O O O O O O O   ↑   O O O O O O O O

O O O O O O O O | O O O O O O O O

O O O O O O O O   O O O O O O O O
                        4 D
O O O O O O O O   3 C   O O O O O O O O
                        2 B
                        1 A
O O O O O O O O   O O O O O O O O

                       P 1stE
O O O O O O O O   E E   O O O O O O O O

The deaconesses (A-D) are standing to the right of the deacons (1-4). The deacons will sit on the front left pew. The deaconesses will sit on the front right pew. The pastor, 1st elder, and two other elders (P, 1st E, E, E) will stand behind the table. The congregation is seated every other pew, beginning at the third pew from the front.

Churches with a Medium or Large Membership

E E E E E E P 1stE E E E E E E

```
┌─────────────────────────────┐
│          Communion          │
│            Table            │
└─────────────────────────────┘
```

7 8 9 10 11 5 12 6		4 3 2 1 A B C D		G M F L K J I H
O O O O		O O O O		O O O O
O O O O		O O O O		O O O O
O O O O	↑	O O O O	↑	O O O O
O O O O		O O O O		O O O O
O O O O		O O O O		O O O O
O O O O	7 1	O O O O A H		O O O O
O O O O	8 2	O O O O B I		O O O O
O O O O	9 3	O O O O C J		O O O O
O O O O	10 4	O O O O D K		O O O O
O O O O	11 5	O O O O F L		O O O O
O O O O	12 6	O O O O G M		O O O O
O O O O		O O O O		O O O O
O O O O	P	O O O O 1stE		O O O O
O O O O	E E	O O O O E E		O O O O
O O O O	E E	O O O O E E		O O O O
O O O O	E E	O O O O E E		O O O O
O O O O		O O O O		O O O O

The deacons (1-12) are paired off in the center left aisle followed by the pastor and six elders (P, E). The deaconesses (A-M) are paired off in the center right aisle followed by the first elder and six elders (1stE, E). The pastor and elders will stand behind the table. The deacons will sit on the left front pew and left half of the center pew. The deaconesses will sit on the right front pew and right half of the center pew.

Deacons Serving Congregation Diagrams

Churches with a Small Membership

E   P   1ST E   E

```
┌─────────────────────────────┐
│         Communion           │
│           Table             │
└─────────────────────────────┘
```

4   3   2   1

A B C D

         4   1

O O O O O O O O   O O O O O O O O

O O O O O O O O   O O O O O O O O

O O O O O O O O   O O O O O O O O
         3   2
O O O O O O O O   O O O O O O O O

O O O O O O O O   O O O O O O O O

O O O O O O O O   O O O O O O O O

When the pastor nods, the deacons (1-4) stand and march to the table to receive the bread trays from the elders behind the table. When the pastor nods again, they take their positions to serve the congregation. Deacons 1 and 4 serve the front half of the church and deacons 2 and 3 serve the back half of the church. After serving the congregation, they follow the agreed upon option listed in "Points to Remember," items 9-11. Repeat for serving wine and collecting glasses.

Churches with a Medium or Large Membership

E E E E E E P 1stE E E E E E E

```
┌─────────────────────────┐
│        Communion         │
│          Table           │
└─────────────────────────┘
```

7 8 9 10 11 5 12 6 4 3 2 1

	A B C D		G M F L K J I H	
8 O O O O 10	5 O O O O 12	4 O O O O 2
O O O O	O O O O	O O O O
O O O O	O O O O	O O O O
O O O O	O O O O	O O O O
O O O O	O O O O	O O O O
O O O O	O O O O	O O O O
O O O O	O O O O	O O O O
O O O O	O O O O	O O O O
7 O O O O 9	11 O O O O 6	3 O O O O 1
O O O O	O O O O	O O O O
O O O O	O O O O	O O O O
O O O O	O O O O	O O O O
O O O O	O O O O	O O O O
O O O O	O O O O	O O O O
O O O O	O O O O	O O O O
O O O O	O O O O	O O O O

When the pastor nods, the deacons (1-12) stand and march to the table to receive the trays from the elders behind the table. When the pastor nods again, they take their positions to serve the congregation. Deacons 2, 4, 12, 5, 10, and 8 serve the front half of the church. Deacons 1, 3, 6, 11, 9, and 7 serve the back half of the church. After serving the congregation, they follow the agreed upon option listed in "Points to Remember," items 9-11. Repeat for serving wine and collecting glasses.

The Lord's Supper Recessional Diagrams

Churches with a Small Membership

```
┌─────────────────────────┐
│      Communion          │
│        Table            │
└─────────────────────────┘
```

```
─────────────────              ↓              ─────────────────
─────────────────                             ─────────────────
O O O O O O O O                               O O O O O O O O

─────────────────                             ─────────────────
O O O O O O O O                               O O O O O O O O

─────────────────        P 1ˢᵗE               ─────────────────
O O O O O O O O          E  E                 O O O O O O O O
─────────────────        4  D                 ─────────────────
O O O O O O O O          3  C                 O O O O O O O O
─────────────────        2  B                 ─────────────────
O O O O O O O O          1  A                 O O O O O O O O

─────────────────                             ─────────────────
O O O O O O O O                               O O O O O O O O
```

After the closing hymn and benediction, the pastor nods for the deacons (1-4) and deaconesses (A-D) to stand and march out in pairs as during the processional. The elders (E) behind the table will follow, then the pastor and first elder (P, 1ˢᵗE).

Churches with a Medium or Large Membership

```
┌─────────────────────────────┐
│          Communion          │
│            Table            │
└─────────────────────────────┘
```

O O O O		O O O O		O O O O
O O O O	↓	O O O O	↓	O O O O
O O O O		O O O O		O O O O
O O O O		O O O O		O O O O
O O O O		O O O O		O O O O
O O O O	P	O O O O	1stE	O O O O
O O O O	E E	O O O O	E E	O O O O
O O O O	E E	O O O O	E E	O O O O
O O O O	E E	O O O O	E E	O O O O
O O O O	7 8	O O O O	I H	O O O O
O O O O	9 10	O O O O	K J	O O O O
O O O O	11 1	O O O O	A L	O O O O
O O O O	5 2	O O O O	B F	O O O O
O O O O	12 3	O O O O	C M	O O O O
O O O O	6 4	O O O O	D G	O O O O
O O O O		O O O O		O O O O

After the closing hymn and benediction, the pastor nods for the deacons (1-12) and deaconesses (A-M) to stand and march out in pairs as during the processional. The elders (E) behind the table will follow, then the pastor and first elder (P, 1stE).

CHAPTER 19

The Ministry of Visitation

The instruction given in the *Church Manual* concerning the visitation of members is: "An important duty belonging to deacons is that of visiting church members in their homes. In many churches this is arranged by a distribution of membership by districts, assigning a deacon to each district, with the expectation that he will visit each home at least once a quarter."[22] Although this duty is   listed as a responsibility of the deaconesses, I recommend that they also participate.

Some of the reasons for visitation are: to become better acquainted with the membership; strengthen new members and absentee members; reclaim backsliders; call on the sick and shut-ins; identify and follow-up on the needs of the elderly, disabled, widows, and single parents (such as house cleaning, yard work, meals, transportation, child care, home weatherization, and other improvements); address family crisis (such as spiritual problems, disaster, illness, domestic violence, bereavement, marital problems, financial problems, and children's behavioral problems); and encourage faithfulness in matters of stewardship.

The Visit

1. Visit in twos: One will pray silently while the other is conversing. A husband wife team is the ideal for visitation, in that the male and female perspectives are represented. However, teams may consist of two deacons; two deaconesses; a deacon and his spouse; a deaconess and her spouse; a deacon and an elder; a deacon and a male church member; and a deaconess and a female church member. In rare situations when a male and female that are not married to each other visit together, they are to use every

---

[22]General Conference of Seventh-day Adventists, *Church Manual*, 57.

safeguard that they can to guard against any of Satan's false accusations.

2. Dress appropriately: Deacons should wear a coat and tie. If the weather is too hot for a coat, shirt and tie should be worn. Deaconesses should be modestly attired in a dress or skirt and blouse.

3. Visiting the Home: State the purpose of the visit upon entering the home—to represent the church and the pastoral staff's concern for the family. It is best to call and schedule visits. However, don't be afraid to "drop by." Unscheduled, spontaneous visits can also be a blessing.

4. The Spirit of the Visit: Pray before entering the home, and maintain the attitude of prayer throughout the visit. It is not a social visit but a spiritual visit.

5. The Nature of the Conversation: Try to assess the needs of the family. Engage them in conversation about their home, the church, their community, their employment, members of their family, and themselves. Document your assessment of the family's needs on a Membership Visitation Form (see example forms at end of chapter). "Be swift to hear, slow to speak, slow to wrath" (Jas 1:19). Don't gossip, nor listen to gossip. Don't take sides when family members disagree. Don't try to defend the pastor, church officer, or member with whom the family may have some differences. Stay objective and assure them that you will join them in prayer for the situation.

6. Length of Visit: Most visits should be about 15-25 minutes. However, in extenuating circumstances, the visit may take longer.

7. Completing the Visit: The closing conversation should be deeply spiritual, and ended with prayer. Respectfully ask that radios or televisions be turned down or off before you begin to pray. The prayer should be brief, but comprehensive enough to include the needs discussed during the visit. Call the family members by name in your prayer. After you have prayed, leave promptly.

8. Review the information that was placed on the Membership Visitation Forms at the end of the day and fill out a Visitation and Outreach Referral Form on each family that has needs. Keep a copy of each form that you fill out for your records and give a copy to the leader of the ministry that can meet the family's needs, the personal ministries leader, and the pastor. After the

leader meets the needs, he/she gives a copy of the completed form to the deacon, deaconess, or elder that made the visit, the personal ministries leader, and the pastor. The deacon, deaconess, or elder is to check with the leader to make sure that the families' needs are met in a timely manner.

The Problem-Solving Process

Naomi I. Brill explains the social systems approach to solving problems in the following manner:

> A family is a system characterized by intimate and specialized relationships. Usually the crisis that precipitates the need for help comes as a problem of an individual family member, a child failing in school or involved in delinquent behavior, a father who cannot hold a job, a mother who drinks heavily, an interfering grandparent, a marriage that is unhappy and deteriorating. The balance within this malfunctioning family is based on the behavior of the troubled family member, and the system will tend to pressure this member to continue in that role. Any change within the member apart from the system is extremely difficult to maintain. While the worker may help on an individual basis, focus should be on work with the family as a whole in order to change the family system and give the individual a fighting chance for healthy behavior.[23]

Based upon this statement, we can better understand why sometimes our best efforts turn out to be a "band-aid." It is important that deacons and deaconesses understand the problem-solving process within the context of the social systems approach. This will enable them to become more effective in making assessments during their visitations, and in providing quality care for families in crisis.

The problem-solving process is a method that is commonly used in the social work discipline. It is a systematic approach used to

---

[23]Naomi I. Brill, *Working with People: The Helping Process*, 2nd ed. (New York: J. B. Lippincott Co., 1978), 86.

empower persons with problems to become actively involved in developing a plan of action toward a solution. There are nine steps to this process. They are practical and relevant and can be used by deacons and deaconesses as they do their visitation. I have redefined the steps to relate to the ministry context. These are the nine steps:

1. Engagement: During the visitation, establish objective and open communication with as many members of the family as possible. This will assist you in formulating preliminary hypotheses (assumptions) for the problem.
2. Assessment: Appraise the situation based upon factual information presented by family members and others familiar with situation; the family's feelings and belief system; and other circumstances.
3. Definition: Work with the family to define the immediate problem, the underlying cause of the immediate problem, and the factors that are standing in the way of finding a prevention.
4. Set Goals: With input from the family, set some realistic goals. This step is most effective when the family has the greater voice in deciding what needs to be achieved and how it should be done.
5. Alternatives: Look at all of the possible ways of addressing the problem and select the best one(s).
6. Contract: Establish an agreement about the roles and responsibilities of each participant. Everyone is to be held accountable.
7. Action: Take steps toward achieving goals.
8. Evaluation: Evaluate the outcome of the action to determine whether or not it was successful.
9. Continuation: Continue to follow the working plan modifying it as needed.[24]

By utilizing the problem-solving process in visitation, deacons and deaconesses will be better equipped to provide quality care for families in crisis. They will have a greater awareness of the church's responsibility to have an equitable system in place for meeting the

---

[24]Ibid., 91.

needs of the members that are poor and sick. As they visit and assess the physical, social, emotional, and spiritual needs of the church members they will seek ways to meet them. This will require the deacons and deaconesses to become knowledgeable of the available resources in the church and in the community, and know the proper steps to take in order to obtain these resources. They are to educate the members in need on what community agencies they can go to for help and how to apply for help.

The church may decide to organize an interdisciplinary team to assist in providing quality care for members in crisis situations. Here are some suggestions for accomplishing this:

1. See that deacons, deaconesses, and elders are trained to apply the problem-solving process in the framework of the social systems approach in visitation.

2. The interdisciplinary team is to consist of a medical physician, nurse, social worker, home health aide, chaplain, financial advisor, substance abuse counselor, and a marriage counselor. Depending upon the needs of the church, other professionals may be added or used in place of these.

3. When the deacons, deaconesses, and elders discover families in crisis through visitation, they would give a copy of their assessment to the team's social worker.

4. The social worker would counsel with the family, develop a plan for intervention, and meet with the other members of the team.

5. Based upon the situation, the team would network within the church and community to assist the family in resolving the problem. (See ecogram at end of chapter as an example of church and community resources for networking)

MEMBERSHIP VISITATION FORM

Visited by _____ Date _____

1. Member's name _____ Phone _____
    Address _____
2. Best time to visit? _____
3. Do I need to call before coming?   ___Yes No___
4. How long have you been a member of this church? _____
5. What do you like best about this church? _____
    _____
6. Does everyone in your family have a Bible?   ___Yes No___
7. Are Sabbath school quarterlies in the home?   ___Yes No___
8. Do you own any Spirit of Prophecy books?   ___Yes No___
9. Are all members of the family baptized SDAs?___Yes No___
10. Is there family worship in the home daily?   ___Yes No___
11. Are the children in church school?   ___Yes No___
    Circle grade level: Elementary   High school   College
12. Is a spouse missing from the home?   ___Yes No___
    Which? _____
13. Do you understand tithes and offerings?   ___Yes No___
14. Have you taught your children to tithe?   ___Yea No___
15. Do any members of the family need work?   ___Yes No___
         Who? _____ Type of work?_____
16. Are you employed?   ___Yes No___
    Where?_____ How long?_____
17. Are you having Sabbath employment problems?__Yes No___
18. List the names and ages of your family. Circle SDA if they are
    members.
    _____   _____
    SDA
    _____   _____
    SDA
    _____   _____
    SDA
19. Family's Needs Assessment: _____
    _____
    _____
    _____

VISITATION AND OUTREACH REFERRAL FORM

Member's name _____

Address _____ City _____

State _____ Zip _____ Telephone ( )_____

Event and date of event: _____

_____

_____

_____

Ministry(s) needed: _____

_____

_____

Member's need(s) referred to _____ Outreach Ministry

Date of referral _____

Referral made by: _____ Telephone ( )_____

....

Ministry(s) provided: _____

_____

_____

_____

Date provided _____

Comments: _____

_____

_____

_____

_____

Person(s) who provided the ministry(s):

_____ Telephone ( )_____

_____ Telephone ( )_____

_____ Telephone ( )_____

(After both sections are completed, give a copy to the
pastor, personal ministries leader, & visiting officer)

PERSONAL INFORMATION SHEET

Name _____ Telephone ( )_____
City _____ State _____ Zip _____
Occupation _____ Employer _____
Date of birth _____

Children Names   Birthday

_____   _____
_____   _____
_____   _____

Public Service Record

Military _____ Business _____

Other organizations _____
_____

Previous Church Experience (check)

___ Church officer or committee member
___ Church school worker
___ Teacher
___ Secretarial
___ Music   ___ vocalist   ___ instrumentalist
        what instrument? _____

___ Outreach ministries (describe) _____

Please check inreach and outreach ministries in which you are interested in working:

Inreach Ministry

Sabbath School
___ Teaching
___ Music
___ Greeter
___ Usher
___ Other _____

Class Levels
___ Cradle Roll
___ Kindergarten
___ Primary
___ Junior
___ Earliteen
___ Youth
___ Adult
___ Extension Division
(Shut-ins)

Outreach Ministry

Vacation Bible School
___ Counselor or craft
___ Teach or help
___ Transportation

Personal Ministries
___ Children Story Hour
___ Communications
___ Community Services
___ Health Education
___ Lay Bible Ministry
___ Nutrition Classes
___ Tracts and Literature
___ Visitation and Prayer
___ Witnessing and Bible Studies
___ Other _____

ECOGRAM

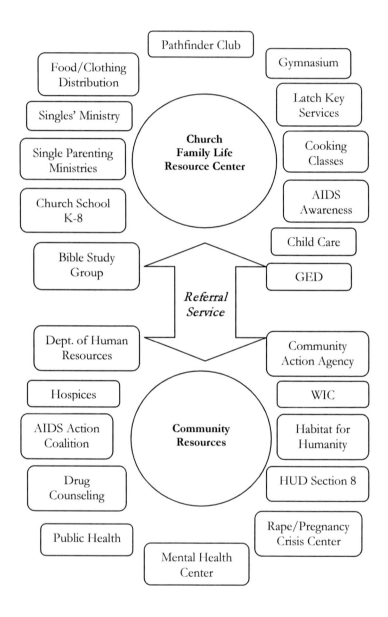

CHAPTER 20

Deacons and Deaconesses as Physical Plant Managers

The Seventh-day Adventist *Church Manual* and the *Manual for Church Officers* present a vivid description of the deacons' responsibilities in regards to maintaining the church properties. When the deacons perceive this work as being an opportunity to witness for God, they will count doing it a privilege. The *Manual for Church Officers* states:

> The appearance of church properties, both the yard and environs, as well as the buildings, bears a striking witness not only to those who enter but to the community at large. Far more people drive by the church than enter in, and their concept of the people who worship within may be largely drawn from the appearance without. An unkempt yard overrun with weeds, or a lawn not properly mowed, will bear an unfavorable testimony. The deacon's pride in his church and concern for its witness will not permit this to happen. His care of church properties will include the following:
>
> 1. Oversee the janitorial work, being certain that the church, including the grounds, is well cared for. It may be necessary at times, as in the spring, for the deacons to arrange for a general work bee [members organized to clean and fix-up] at the church. Under proper supervision, much can be accomplished in a few hours.
> 2. See to such needed repairs as broken windows, plumbing, lighting, and heating.
> 3. Bring to the church board or finance committee suggestions for major repairs and improvements.
> 4. See to the care and proper distribution of the church hymnals in the sanctuary. Have them properly placed, front facing the worshiper and right side up, in the hymn racks. Keep the racks free from litter.

5. Have the offering envelopes properly placed in the racks.
6. Have the pulpit furniture properly placed, micro-phones checked, and everything in order for services.
7. Open the church building before each regular meeting, and lock the doors after the service is concluded.[25]

In areas that overlap with the work of the ushers, deacons and deaconesses should seek to have a harmonious relationship with them and work out a schedule that will allow for the sharing of these responsibilities.

It is important to note that although the deacons are the primary ones responsible for the upkeep of the church properties, they do not have to do all of the work themselves. They may request a budget from the church to contract it out or use volunteer help. The *Church Manual* addresses this issue by saying, "In large churches it is often necessary to employ a janitor. The deacons should recommend a suitable person to the church board, which takes action by vote to employ such help, or the church board may authorize the deacons to employ a janitor."[26]

Remember, first and foremost, the deacons' calling is a spiritual calling. Although they are responsible for multiple tasks in the church, they are not to be distracted from their number one goal of winning souls and nurturing the membership.

In some churches the building committee is responsible for seeing that the church is clean and the temperature is appropriately set. But even when this is the case, Naylor states:

> Deacons, however, as officials of the church are to have an interest in the building and take pride therein. If the building is not warm enough and no one is doing anything about it, the deacon should be the first one to arise quietly and see that something is done. All of the deacons should be alert to the details of the building appointments when they arrive on

[25]General Conference of Seventh-day Adventists, *Manual for Church Officers*, 85.

[26]General Conference of Seventh-day Adventists, *Church Manual*, 71-72.

Sunday [Saturday/Sabbath] morning.

To wait until the service is under way to make criticisms or adjustments is to wait too long. It could be that it is the particular responsibility of some of the deacons to serve on the building committee and to tend to these matters that are suggested.[27]

The *Manual for Church Officers* gives some specific instructions to deacons for providing a comfortable atmosphere in the church for those who come to worship. It states:

Although we can cite instances in which worshipers have been glad for the privilege of worship even amid most rigorous and uncomfortable circumstances, still it is true that one's comfort may affect the spiritual blessings received and may even determine whether some worshipers will return. Comfort has much to do with providing the proper atmosphere for worship. Visitors especially will react quickly. Church comfort will include the following:

1. Ensuring proper heating [and cooling] of building before each service.
2. Maintaining proper heat and ventilation. Frigid conditions are distracting; too warm a temperature will contribute to drowsiness.
3. Ensuring proper lighting. Burned-out bulbs should be replaced before the next service. Proper illumination, highlighting the pulpit area, the communion table with the open Bible, et cetera, can add much to the atmosphere of worship. Poor lighting, with the subsequent drab effect, can create real barriers to worship. Entering a well-lighted sanctuary is similar to being warmly and cordially welcomed.
4. Seeing that all supplies are complete, such as towels, soap, and toilet tissue. Special attention should be given to assure that bathrooms are clean and wastebaskets empty.

---

[27]Naylor, 85.

5. Checking carefully at each service to see that nothing is lying about to mar the appearance, such as litter on the shelves above the coat racks or on the back pews, the communion table, piano, or window sills. Everything should be in top condition for a meeting with the Master. Also, clean out the pulpit regularly.

6. Taking special note of visitors and newcomers to the church, making sure that they are comfortably seated and that they have hymnals.

7. Providing for proper ushering. It is advisable that persons other than the deacons act as ushers. These can include younger men [and women] and those newer in the faith, and the experience can be useful training for their later work as deacons [or deaconesses]. The deacons [and deaconesses], however, should have the skills of a good usher and will at times be called upon to serve as such. The deacons [and deaconesses] and ushers should be given special instructions so that they can perform this important duty with aptitude and grace. The congregation may need education as to how to respond to the helpfulness of the ushers. Even in small churches, ushering can add much in the way of dignity and blessing of a service. The use of badges to identify the ushers and deacons [and deaconesses] will help to ease their work.

8. Helping to maintain reverence. Worshipers should not be seated at times when it would detract from the service. Asterisks can be placed in the bulletin to indicate the appropriate times. Maintaining reverence will include tact and wisdom in situations that may arise in the case of disturbances by intruders, cases of epilepsy, or even boisterous youth. It may also involve inviting children or youth into the services who may be running about in the halls and rooms. [28]

It may be necessary to have boisterous youth and children that are running in the halls and rooms to sit with their parents or other adult.

---

[28]General Conference of Seventh-day Adventists, *Manual for Church Officers*, 85-86.

Deacons and deaconesses that are not scheduled to serve during a particular service should assist with these situations. I would suggest this as a rule of thumb, although a deacon or deaconess is not scheduled to be on duty, he or she is never off duty. A situation that occurs at the back of the sanctuary, in the foyer, rest room, class room, or the parking lot is better handled by a deacon or deaconess that is not on duty seated on the front pew.

Although the sources that provided the above lists of responsibilities directed their focus on deacons, I propose that deaconesses should assist in those areas of physical plant management that are within the range of their physical capabilities.

Fellowship Dinners

"At fellowship dinners, unless the responsibility is assigned to others, deaconesses should care for the arranging of the food, clean-up, and other needs that may arise."[29]

"The deacons should see that the tables and chairs are properly arranged, and assist in their removal or rearrangement after the dinner."[30] They should also see to it that spills and trash are properly cared for. Also, they should make certain that the elderly are seated and served in a timely manner.

---

[29]Ibid., 100.

[30]Ibid., 89.

.

CHAPTER 21

Organizing a Telephone Committee

A vast number of people spend a lot of time talking on the telephone. However, it is seldom regarded as a tool with which to conduct a viable ministry in the church. Perhaps this is due to the inordinate amount of time that people talk on the telephone, while neglecting their work. Ellen White gave some inspired counsel against this. She stated: "Let no one lose minutes by talking when he should be working. Let the talkative man remember that there are times when he has no right to talk. Close your lips. Make not others idle by tempting them to listen to your talk. The time of many is lost when a man uses his tongue instead of his tools."[31]

In spite of the negative press that the telephone has received, opportunities should be sought for positive ways to use it for ministry. One positive way is to organize a telephone committee in the church. This is a ministry that the deacons and deaconesses may want to consider establishing.

The Focus of the Committee

This committee should have two focus areas. These areas are inreach and outreach. Inreach refers to ministries that nurture church members by meeting their spiritual, physical, and emotional needs. Outreach refers to ministries that nurture non-church members by meeting their spiritual, physical, and emotional needs. Listed below are ways in which a telephone committee can minister to both of these areas:

INREACH

1. Call sick and shut-in members
2. Call elderly members

---

[31]Ellen White, *Evangelism*, 653-654.

3. Call bereaved members
4. Call members on special occasions, such as birthday, wedding anniversary, birth of a child, graduation, job promotions, etc.
5. Call members on Friday nights to wish a "Happy Sabbath" and to encourage Sabbath school attendance.
6. Call members going through difficult trials
7. Call pastor and general membership
8. Call absent members
    a. Let them know that they are missed. Encourage them to return.
    b. Find out areas of ministries needed to facilitate their return.

OUTREACH

1. Call people who visit the church for divine worship on Sabbath, and for other church services. Express appreciation for their visit, and invite them back.
2. Call people in your area who are on the Adventist media programs' interest lists (Breath Of Life, Voice Of Prophecy, It Is Written). Take a telephone survey, and set up an appointment for a home visit.
3. Call people located in the church's evangelistic meeting target area to inform them of the meeting and invite them to come.
4. Call people who visit the evangelistic meetings, and invite them to return the following evening. When they are absent, call and let them know that they were missed.
5. Call friends, relatives, and neighbors to keep them informed of special church activities.

Who Should Serve on the Committee?

It is important that those who serve on this committee meet certain qualifications. This is an important ministry and the members of this committee must have a high level of sensitivity toward people and a kind spirit. This ministry requires, as Jim Collins proposes, that the right people are on the bus in the right seats.[32]

1. Members with pleasant personalities
2. Focused individuals
3. Members who express positive views of the church
4. Members who are spiritual
5. Non-gossipers
6. Good listeners
7. Non-debaters
8. Members who have the time (homebound; home-makers; retirees; part time workers)

HOW TO ORGANIZE THE COMMITTEE

1. The head deacon and head deaconess solicit involvement from members of their board and other church members who fit the above criteria.
2. Identify committee members who would work best in the various areas of Inreach and Outreach.
3. Conduct training sessions.
4. Assign names from church's roll to committee members.
5. Have the committee members who are working in the same area (Inreach/Outreach) to exchange their calling list each quarter.
6. Committee members should keep a file on each person they call. Do not write confidential disclosures shared by the persons called in the file. These files will be passed on along with the calling lists to other committee members.
7. Committee members are to assess areas of ministries needed by those they call, and report it on a Telephone Ministry Referral Form (see Telephone Committee forms at end of chapter).
8. Committee members will meet at least once a quarter to evaluate and monitor their progress. They are to modify the process as needed.

---

[32]Jim Collins, *Good to Great* (New York: HarperCollins Publishers, Inc., 2001), 41.

TELEPHONE MINISTRY REFERRAL FORM

Member's name _____

Address _____ City _____

State _____ Zip _____ Telephone ( )_____

Event and date of event: _____

_____

_____

_____

Ministry(s) needed: _____

_____

_____

Member's need(s) referred to _____ Ministry

Date of referral _____

Referral made by: _____ Telephone ( )_____

....

Ministry(s) provided: _____

_____

_____

_____

Date provided _____

Comments: _____

_____

_____

_____

_____

Person(s) who provided the ministry(s):

_____ Telephone ( )_____

_____ Telephone ( )_____

_____ Telephone ( )_____

(After both sections are completed, give a copy to the
pastor, personal ministries leader, & caller)

TELEPHONE MINISTRY SURVEY
(Adventist Media Interests)

Name _____

Hello! Is this the _____'s residence?
May I speak with Mr./Mrs. _____? Mr./Mrs. _____ my name is
_____ and I am a Field Representative for the _____.

    According to our records, on _____ you enrolled in the
_____Bible Study Course. I am calling to do a follow-up survey. May
I ask you a few questions?   Yes___ No___
Did you enjoy the lessons?   Yes ___ No ___
Have you completed the entire series?   Yes ___ No ___
Do you now understand the Bible better?   Yes ___ No ___
What did you learn from the lessons that you did not know
already?_____
_____

Would you like additional information on this topic? Yes __ No __
What did you like best about the Bible Study Course? _____
_____
What did you like least about the Course? _____
_____
Are you practicing what you have learned?   Yes ___ No ___
Are you telling others what you have learned?   Yes ___ No ___

    Thank you Mr./Mrs. _____ for answering these questions. If
you don't mind, Mr./Mrs. _____, I would like your permission to
have a member of our Visitation Team to come by your home to pray
with you, and to answer any questions that you may have concerning
the Bible. If that's okay, is morning or evening best for you? A.M. ___
P.M. ___. What day? _____. What is your current street address?
_____

    I will pass this information on to our Visitation Team, and have
someone to call you. May I have prayer with you? Pray _____

Retain form, but TRANSFER pertinent information to Telephone Ministry Referral Form

TELEPHONE MINISTRY EVANGELISTIC CANVASS

Hello, is this the _____ 's residence?

I'm Mr./Mrs. _____ with the JESUS IS THE ANSWER EVANGELISTIC CRUSADE. I'm calling to invite you and your family to the meetings that are being held at _____.

By registering each night that you come, you could possibly win one of three gifts that will be given away on the final night of the Crusade. You could win a large Heritage Family Bible; or a beautiful framed picture of Jesus; or a set of 5 books that will help you to better understand the Bible.

The opening night of the Crusade is Saturday, July 10th at 7:00 p.m., and it will end Saturday, July 31st. There will be no meetings on Thursday nights.

If you have children, please bring them with you. We will have Vacation Bible School, which begins at 7:00 also. So while you are enjoying the adult meetings, the children will be doing arts and crafts and listening to children Bible stories in the class rooms just outside of the main auditorium.

Evangelist _____ is an excellent speaker. He will be explaining many of the prophecies of the Bible, especially those found in the books of Daniel and Revelation.

Will you need transportation to the meetings? Yes ___ No ___. May God bless you Mr./Mrs. _____. I'm looking forward to seeing you on opening night of the Crusade. Please ask one of the ushers to let me know that you are there so I can meet you and your family. Here is my telephone number, if you need any assistance in getting to the meetings, _____.

May I have prayer with you? Yes ___ No ___.

Pray _____

Conclusion

The ministry of deacons and deaconesses is a spiritual calling that involves a variety of responsibilities within the church. These officers welcome the members and visitors as they enter the church and assist them find seats when necessary, teach God's Word, collect tithes and offerings, assist the treasurer in counting the funds, attend all of the services of the church and participate in various capacities as needed, visit the members, minister to the bereaved, assist at funerals, fellowship dinners, baptismal and Holy Communion services, maintain the church properties, care for the sick and needy, and minister to members by serving on the telephone committee. Their ministry is multi-faceted and requires dedication and commitment.

PART V

Developing a Ministry for the Twenty-First Century Deacon and Deaconess that Reflects the Biblical Model

Introduction

It is important to educate the members of the church at the beginning of the process of restoring the deacons and deaconesses to their biblical role and function. In order for these officers to succeed in fulfilling their ministry, they need the support of the church members, fellow church officers, pastor, and pastoral staff. Therefore, Part V of this book will provide a strategy for educating the membership concerning the multi-faceted responsibilities of deacons and deaconesses, and to challenge them to become more sensitive and supportive of these officers. The following chapters will also offer a strategy for conducting training workshops and retreats for deacons and deaconesses, and training them to serve as Bible workers in the church. This training will equip them to successfully carry out their responsibilities as the church empowers them. Part V consists of the following chapters:

Therefore, brethren, pick out from among you seven men of good repute, full of the Spirit and of wisdom, whom we may appoint to this duty. But we will devote ourselves to prayer and to the ministry of the word. And the word of God increased; and the number of the disciples multiplied in Jerusalem greatly.

Acts 6:3-4,7 (RSV)

I commend to you our sister Phoebe, a deaconess of the church at Cenchreae, that you may receive her in whatever she may require from you, for she has been a helper of many and of myself as well.

Rom 16:1-2 (RSV)

CHAPTER 22

Preparing the Church to Empower the Deacons and Deaconesses

Before the church is willing to empower the deacons and deaconesses to perform ministry beyond the limited role that has become the norm, the members must have a clear understanding of the theological foundation for change. The job description of the deacons in the first century Christian church was of such a nature that it allowed them the freedom to exercise all of the spiritual gifts that God chose to bestow upon them individually. The church recognized that these officers were a great asset to the gospel work and were willing to empower them to function in a variety of ways.

Ellen G. White made this observation regarding the empowerment of the deacons elected by the first century Christian church: "It is proper for all matters of a temporal nature to come before the proper officers [deacons] and be by them adjusted. But if they are of so difficult a character as to baffle their wisdom, they should be carried into the council of those who have the oversight of the entire church."[1]

The implication of this for the ministry of the deacons and deaconesses of the Seventh-day Adventist church in the twenty-first century is that the pastor, elders, and church members must give deacons and deaconesses a sense of empowerment if they are to fulfill their God-given role. Only when these officers cannot resolve an issue are they to bring it to the pastor or the church board. This kind of empowerment allows deacons and deaconesses the freedom to carry out their responsibilities with courage and dignity without having to say, "The Pastor said," in order to get the cooperation of members. When the pastor uses his influence from the pulpit and in other ways to solicit the members' cooperation for the deacons and deaconesses, it informs the congregation that the pastor and officers work as a team. This also helps to establish a sense of empowerment among the deacons and deaconesses.

---

[1] Ellen G. White, *The Story of Redemption*, 261.

Therefore, I recommend that once the pastor embraces the concept of restoring the deacons and deaconesses to their biblical role and function, that he initiates the process by presenting a series of Sabbath sermons entitled The Life of the Early Church. These seven sermons are developed from the Book of Acts and should be presented starting the month of January of the year that the church is scheduled to elect new officers. The purpose for starting early in the election year is to allow enough time to train those interested in serving as deacons and deaconesses so they will be qualified to be elected. The goal is to highlight the principles that the members of the first century Christian church used that caused it to grow spiritually and numerically, and to challenge the church members to implement those principles. Those principles are found in Acts 2:42, 46, and 47:

> And they continued stedfastly in the apostles' doctrine and fellowship, and in breaking of bread, and in prayers. And they, continuing daily with one accord in the temple, and breaking bread from house to house, did eat their meat with gladness and singleness of heart, praising God, and having favour with all the people. And the Lord added to the church daily such as should be saved.

The pastor is to challenge the membership to apply these principles by reading and studying the Bible daily, and following the doctrines taught by the Seventh-day Adventist church; visiting, calling, and inviting each other home for supper during the week; attending all of the services of the church, opening the church during the week for prayer, praise, and worship services; having family worship in the mornings and evenings in their homes; developing an effective prayer life, calling each other for prayer, praying with co-workers and neighbors, and praying for people they want to be saved.

At the conclusion of the first sermon, which deals with the need for prayer and the power of the Holy Spirit to become effective witnesses for Jesus, the pastor should make an appeal to those interested in becoming prayer warriors for the church. Those who sign up are to pair off and develop a schedule to come to the church, or some other location, at certain times during the week to pray. These prayer warriors should meet and identify the focus areas that all of them will be praying for. Here are some examples of focus areas to pray for:

PRAYER FOCUS AREAS

1. Outpouring of the Holy Spirit
2. Revival and reformation in the church
3. Unity in the church
4. Nurturing the members
5. Youth and young adults
6. Senior citizens
7. Home bound members
8. Faithfulness in stewardship
9. Health reform among members
10. Unsaved family members
11. Relatives of other faiths
12. Wisdom to use Christ's method alone
13. Community's receptivity to the gospel
14. Discernment to work for the community
15. Identify and use of spiritual gifts

Here is an example of the prayer warriors' weekly schedule:

PRAYER WARRIORS' SCHEDULE

Day and Time	Warriors Name	Location
Sunday		
4:00-5:00 a.m.	___, ___	Home
Monday		
8:15-9:15 a.m.	___, ___	Church
12:00-1:00 p.m.	___, ___, ___	Church
5:00-6:00 p.m.	___, ___	Church
6:30-7:30 p.m.	___, ___	Church
Tuesday		
8:15-9:15 a.m.	___, ___	Church
10:00-12:00 p.m.	___, ___	Church
12:00-2:00 p.m.	___, ___, ___	Church
6:30-7:30 p.m.	___, ___	Church

Wednesday

8:15-9:15 a.m.	____, ____	Church
10:00-12:00 p.m.	____, ____, ____	Church
12:00-1:00 p.m.	Noon Prayer Meeting	Church
6:00-7:00 p.m.	____, ____	Church
7:00-8:00 p.m.	Evening Prayer Meeting	Church

Thursday

8:15-9:15 a.m.	____, ____	Church
12:00-1:00 p.m.	____, ____	Church
5:30-6:30 p.m.	____, ____	Church
6:30-7:30 p.m.	____, ____	Church

Friday

8:15-9:15 a.m.	____, ____	Church
12:00-1:00 p.m.	____, ____	Church

Sabbath (Divine Worship)

1st Sabbaths	____, ____	Church
2nd Sabbaths	____, ____	Church
3rd Sabbaths	____, ____	Church
4th Sabbaths	____, ____	Church
5th Sabbaths	____, ____	Church

Sermon Series

There are seven sermons in this series. The pastor may choose to present more or less. The idea is to communicate to the church members the principles that the members of the early church followed, and to make them relevant to church in the twenty-first century.

The sixth sermon is taken from Acts 6, which deals with the call and ministry of the first deacons. This sermon is to be used as a means to educate the membership concerning the multi-faceted responsibilities of the deacons and deaconesses, and to challenge them to become more sensitive and supportive of these officers. At the conclusion of the sermon, the pastor should invite everyone who is currently serving as a deacon or deaconess, and those who are interested in serving to meet with him immediately after service to sign up to participate in a training workshop.

The following sermon outlines can be used in the process of educating the church membership:

THE LIFE OF THE EARLY CHURCH

Sermon #1 Can I Get a Witness? (Acts 1:1-11)

Luke, the author of the Book of Acts, addressed his writing to Theophilus. It is believed that Theophilus was one of Luke's converts that he had won to Christ. Luke was a witness.

I.   During the forty days that Jesus was with His apostles following His resurrection, He discussed with them their need to be baptized with the Holy Ghost. This was not an option if they were to accomplish their mission to evangelize the world by their witness (Acts 1:4-5).

      A.   The church's mission today is still to evangelize the world through its witness.

      B.   The success of our mission also depends upon the baptism of the Holy Ghost.

II.   The apostles were more concerned about their situation— Rome had authority over them—than they were about witnessing (Acts 1:6).

      A.   Jesus wanted them to receive Holy Ghost Power to change the world, but they wanted power to change their situation so that they would have authority over Rome.

      B.   Church members today also seem to be more concerned with authority and control issues than about receiving the power of the Holy Ghost to witness.

III.   It was not for the apostles to know when God would deal with Rome (Acts 1:7).

      A.   God did not promise the apostles or us power to change our situations. We must leave our situations in His hands.

        B.   God promised to give His apostles and us Power to witness! Not power to change our situations, but power to change the world (Acts 1:8)

IV.   After the apostles received Holy Ghost Power, the first item on their agenda was to get another witness. "One must be ordained to be a witness with us of His resurrection" (Acts 1:22).

        A.   When we as a church receive Holy Ghost Power, the first item on our agenda will be to get another witness.

        B.   God is always trying to get another witness! Will we be His witnesses today? God is asking, "Can I Get a Witness?"

V.   Acts 1:14 tells us what it takes for us to become witnesses.

        A.   Get on one accord

        B.   Be consistent in prayer

        C.   Be consistent in supplication.

VI.   Appeals–Be a witness; join Prayer Warriors' Ministry; accept Christ; join the church.

Sermon #2 **Look on Us (Acts 3:1-11)**

Several months after Pentecost, the members of the early church were still excited about their faith. They continued daily to follow the apostles' doctrine; to fellowship in breaking of bread from house to house; to worship in the temple; and to offer up prayers. This is the NT model for individual spiritual growth and for church growth.

    I.   Peter and John and the other disciples put prayer and worship first. They didn't have to make time for prayer and worship. Prayer and worship were the main activities of their day.

        A.   They went to the temple every day at 9:00 in the morning and 3:00 in the afternoon—the third and ninth hours (Acts 3:1).

        B.   Like Peter and John, every time we come to church, we pass people who have been crippled by life's circumstances. God places some of them in our path, and Satan places some of them in our path. But either way, they are placed there to test us.

C. They look on us expecting something (Acts 3:2-5). Dr. Maurice Riley says, "Today in the confused and cruel world in which we live, many people are hurting and need to be comforted. Hurting, due to loneliness, hurting because of disappointments, heartbreaks over broken homes, hurting because of the sickness of a love-one, perhaps an incurable alcohol or substance abusing relative in the home, disobedient children, and just plain 'hard to make ends meet' syndromes. Sometimes these hurting souls are right in church with us. Many times they are our next door neighbors. They see us rushing out to church, apparently happy, content, and carefree, all dressed in our white attire, and never even tarry long enough to say: 'Come go with me.' Deaconesses must reach out for those 'hurting ones' and serve as God's 'angels of mercy' in an era of ruthlessness and selfishness. Someone is waiting for our outreached hand of compassion, love and mercy."[2]

II. Peter and John introduced this crippled man to the ministry of healing.

A. God has given the Health Message to this church so we can tell the sick to "Look on us!"

B. As we follow the NT model, God will fill us with Holy Ghost Power, and we will be able to minister to people outside the church in such a powerful way that they will come inside the church to praise God with us (Acts 3:8).

III. Appeal–Power to tell others to "Look on you" so you can minister to their physical need and then lead them to Jesus.

---

[2]Riley, 34.

Sermon #3 **Principles of Witnessing Used by the Early Church: Part 1 (Acts 3:11-21)**

The impact that was made by Peter and John's ministry to the lame man was phenomenal. God used that one single event to reach a larger audience. This teaches us to never underestimate the value of ministering to one soul. There are ten principles that Peter and John used as they continued to witness about Jesus. Here are five of those principles.

I.   When God sees fit to use us, give Him the glory (Acts 3:12-13).
   A.   God allowed Peter and John to see some immediate results from their witnessing because He could trust them to give Him the glory.
   B.   The early church grew because they gave glory to God.

II.   Confront sin (Acts 3:13-15)
   A.   There comes a time when we witness for Jesus that we must confront people about their sins. We are to do it in a loving way. But we must not allow them to feel comfortable living in sin.
   B.   Our message is a call to Fear God and give glory to Him; to worship Him; get ready for judgment; and come out of Babylon, and give up Babylonian ways (Rev 14:6-12).

III.   Exalt Jesus (Acts 3:16)
   A.   Make Jesus the center of our witness. Exalt Jesus above church doctrine.
   B.   The Sabbath without Jesus is a boring day of prohibitions. The State of the Dead means nothing without the Resurrection and Second Coming of Jesus.

IV.   Show empathy (Acts 3:17)
   A.   Peter told the Jews that they killed Jesus out of ignorance. Some of the people that we witness to are committing sins out of ignorance, just like we use to. Therefore, let them know that we can identify with them

  B. God gives all a chance to know better so we can do better (Acts 17:30).

V. Make an appeal and give hope (Acts 3:19-21)

  A. We must not be afraid to extend an appeal to those we witness to.

  B. Get a decision by asking them: "Do you believe what God's Word is saying about your lifestyle? Do you believe that Jesus died to offer you a better way of living? Are you willing to accept His offer today by repenting of your sins and allowing Him to change you?"

VI. Appeal–Be committed to apply these principles in your witnessing for Jesus

Sermon #4 Principles of Witnessing Used by the Early Church: Part 2 (Acts 4:1-13)

When we follow these principles in witnessing for Jesus, two things are guaranteed to happen: (1) we will be persecuted (Acts 4:3; 2 Tim 3:12), and (2) somebody will believe in Jesus (Acts 4:4; Isa 55:11). The next five principles are as follows:

VII. Be bold for Jesus (Acts 4:13)

  A. The persecutors didn't have a case, so they tried to bluff Peter and John (Acts 4:14-18).

  B. Those who challenge our faith are usually bluffing also. They are hoping that we will back down. They don't have a case against us. They are afraid of our godly influence.

VIII. Be true to God and conscience (Acts 4:19-20)

  A. We are to do what's right in God's sight and not be intimidated by man's threats and bluffs.

  B. Whatever happens when we witness is intended for God's glory, and when it is over, we have a testimony to share.

IX. Give your testimony (Acts 4:23)

  A. When we give our testimony, we encourage others to trust God more.

B.   We gain strength to overcome the devil (Rev 12:11).
X.   Praise God in the face of persecution (Acts 4:24)
    A.   Praise God for the privilege of suffering for Jesus (1 Pet 2:20-21).
    B.   There is a blessing in store for those who suffer for Jesus (Matt 5:10; 2 Tim 2:12).
XI.   Pray for more boldness and power (Acts 4:29-31)
    A.   Peter and John were not satisfied with just one lame man being healed and joining the church, or 3,000 baptisms on Pentecost, or 5,000 baptisms a few months later. They wanted more.
    B.   The early church was about prayer-power and soul-winning. After they prayed and received more power, they won more souls (Acts 5:14).
    C.   God wants us to have this kind of prayer-power and soul-winning experience. We can have it if we follow the model and principles outlined in the book of Acts.
XII.   Appeal–Pray that God will help you to follow these principles to witness and win souls for Jesus

Sermon #5 **Why Lie? (Acts 5:1-11)**

Ananias and Sapphira wanted to be highly favored and recognized by the church like Barnabas and others who gave, but they didn't want to make the sacrifice. They sold some land, kept back part of the money, and gave the rest to the apostles. The Greek word for "kept back" is also used in Joshua 7 (LXX) to describe the sin of Achan. Whenever we keep back our possessions from God under pretense, we are also guilty of the sin of Achan. Keeping part of the money wasn't a sin in itself. In fact, they could have kept all of the money. It was their property and their money. They didn't have to give it; and Peter told them so (Acts 5:4). The sin was that they pretended that they had given the total amount that they had received for the land. They lied.

I.   Peter confronted Ananias while he was giving him the money (Acts 5:3).

      A. When we joined this church, we agreed to support the church with our tithes and offerings. Tithe is 10% of our income. Our offerings should be in proportion to how God is blessing us.

      B. When we write an amount on our envelope for tithes, we are saying that this reflects the total amount of our income. We are saying the same thing that Ananias and Sapphira said, "This is all that I received."

      C. When we do not write or give anything for tithes, we are saying, "We did not receive anything."

II.   Liars did not make it in the early Christian church.

      A. God punished them by death (Acts 5:5-11).

      B. Liars will not make it into the Kingdom of God (Rev. 22:15).

III.   God has many ways of meetings our needs (Phil 4:19).

      A. Withholding our tithes and offerings is not one of those ways (Mal 3:10).

      B. God always has a "ram in the thicket" for us when we trust His (Gen 22:1-13).

IV.   Appeal–Do not lie to God; be a faithful steward

Sermon #6 Deacons and Deaconesses: A Return to the Biblical Model (Acts 6:1-8)

The early church was made up of many classes of people from different nationalities. This was due to the outpouring of the Holy Spirit on the Day of Pentecost. Acts 2 records that the Holy Spirit fell upon many of the dispersed Jews of every nation that had gathered at Jerusalem for this feast day. Among that group, were those commonly known as Grecians or Hellenistic Jews. There was a division between the Grecian Jews and the Palestinian Jews. They were divided by their language and culture. One group spoke Greek and grew up absorbed by the Greek culture. The other group spoke Hebrew or Aramaic and grew up in Palestine. Despite the existing differences of these two groups, the Holy Spirit brought them together in harmony and in love. They were of one accord and had all things in common. They sold what they had and divided it among themselves. They visited each other daily and ate together with gladness and singleness of heart (Acts 2:1, 44-46).

The unity of spirit was short lived as old prejudices of the past resurfaced. Feelings of distrust, jealousy, and suspicion brought about faultfinding and murmuring. Allegations were made that the Grecian widows were being neglected in the "daily ministration."

I.   The Calling of the NT deacons (Acts 6:1-7)
    A.   They were called to serve and to share the responsibility of the work of the church.
    B.   They came into existence because of a problem in the church. They were called to be problem solvers, conflict managers, social workers, and spiritual counselors.
    C.   They preached the gospel and won converts to the church (Acts 6:8-7:60; 8:5-6, 26-40).

II.   Female deacons/deaconesses served in the NT Church (Rom 16:1-2).
    A.   It is believed that Phoebe was a deaconess at the church in Cenchrea.
    B.   The women spoken of in 1 Tim 3:11 were female deacons.
    C.   Their responsibilities during the first five centuries were to: assist the women at baptisms, greet the women parishioners, direct them to their seats, maintain order among them, and care for the sick and needy.[3]

III.   Qualifications of deacons (1 Tim 3:8-13)
    A.   They are to be grave, which means to be worthy of honor or to be dignified.
    B.   They are not to be doubletongued, which means saying one thing to one person and giving a different view of it to someone else.
    C.   They are not to be addicted to wine, which means abstinence.
    D.   They are not to take bribes.

---

[3]Riley, 1.

E. They are to have a connection with God so that He can give them divine revelations of His Word to teach to others.

F. They are to be faithful husbands, not polygamous, or flirtatious. They are to train their children to obey and encourage their spouse to live a godly life.

IV. Today's deacons and deaconesses are the counterparts to the OT Sons of Korah and keepers of the gates (1 Chr 9:19-29).

A. They were the "keepers of the gates of the tabernacle." Deacons and deaconesses carry out this responsibility when they are called upon to usher and maintain order.

B. They lived close by the tabernacle and were responsible for opening the doors every morning for worship. Deacons are responsible for opening and securing the doors before and after services.

C. They rotated their duties from Sabbath to Sabbath. Deacons and deaconesses also schedule and rotate their duties.

D. They worked in the treasury. Deacons collect the tithes and offerings and assist in counting the funds.

E. They oversaw the sacred vessels and instruments of the tabernacle. Deacons and deaconesses are responsible for maintaining inventory of equipment.

F. They were in charge of the fine flour, oil, and wine. Deaconesses use these items in preparing for the Lord's Supper.

V. Appeal–Deacons and deaconesses, be willing to change and follow the biblical model for service.

Sermon #7 How to Turn an Enemy into a Friend? (Acts 9:10-20)

Saul of Tarsus was the most notorious enemy of the early Christian church. He was zealous about his religion but misled. He consented to the stoning death of Stephen, one of the original deacons. Saul reaped havoc on the church. He entered the homes of the Christians and took them to prison. If we were members of the early Christian church, Saul would have been our enemy. How do we turn an enemy like Saul into a friend? The following six principles will help us to accomplish this challenge.

I.   Recognize that when we are being persecuted for living right, our enemy is Jesus' enemy. Therefore, the battle is not ours; it's the Lord's (Acts 9:3-5).
    A. Jesus knows the best way to deal with His enemies.
    B. Jesus wants to turn His enemies into friends instead of destroying them. But He needs our cooperation in order to accomplish this. Ananias cooperated with Jesus.
II. Go and inquire about our enemy (Acts 9:10-11).
    A. Show our enemy that we have a genuine concern for his/her well-being.
    B. Do not distance ourselves and be indifferent. This will perpetuate a cycle of disharmony.
III. Believe that Jesus is already preparing our enemy to receive us as a friend (Acts 9:11-12).
    A. Eventually our enemy will get tired of persecuting us. He/she will have a change of heart.
    B. Sometimes God will take our enemy through hardships so that he/she can become sensitive to the suffering that he/she is causing us. Do not rejoice in his/her suffering; but believe that Jesus is using it to turn him/her into a friend.
IV. Do not listen to or rehearse the negative comments of others concerning our enemy once Jesus has convicted us to pray for him/her (Acts 9:13-14).
    A. Negative thoughts and talk will cause us to doubt Jesus' ability to change our enemy's heart.
    B. It is not about us being persecuted. It is about Jesus saving our persecutor.
V.   Our perception of our enemy will change once we realize that Jesus loves him/her and has chosen him/her for a special work (Acts 9:15-16).
    A. Jesus is no respecter of persons. He wants to save our enemy just like He wants to save us.

B. Our enemy is Jesus' enemy. Jesus wants us to help Him save this enemy.

VI. If we treat our enemy like a brother, he/she will see the Light (Acts 9:17-18).

    A. Our enemy will see Jesus, the Light of the world, in us. He/she will also see his/her need to accept Jesus as Lord and Savior.

    B. Like Ananias, we may be privileged to witness our enemy being baptized into the church.

VII. Appeal–Cooperate with Jesus so He can turn our enemies into friends and members of His church and Kingdom.

Now that the pastor has educated the members of the church by presenting this series of messages, and the prayer warriors are praying for a revival and reformation in the church, he is now ready to take the deacons and deaconesses, and those who are interested in becoming deacons and deaconesses on a weekend training retreat.

CHAPTER 23

Conducting a Training Retreat for Deacons and Deaconesses

A weekend retreat at a resort surrounded by nature can be a tremendous blessing to the deacons and deaconesses. It would be a time for them to bond with each other and with the pastor also. If going to a resort is not feasible, the training can be done on a weekend at the church.

I recommend that the pastor reiterate to the church elders and other officers the purpose of empowering the deacons and deaconesses to return to the biblical model for ministry. The purpose is to equip them to become more effective in working along with the elders as members of the same team in ministering to the church. Having this assurance will minimize the tension that could possibly arise. The pastor may consider inviting the first elder to attend the retreat with them. Upon returning, he could share his experience with the other elders, and encourage them to support the concept.

The pastor should have a joint meeting with the deacons and deaconesses and share his burden to support them in their ministry. He should ask them how they would feel about going on a training retreat. The purpose of the retreat would be to seek God's vision for the deacon and deaconess board, develop a vision and a mission statement, and establish goals and objectives. If they agree, ask them for suggestions about the location and dates. The pastor along with these officers may decide on inviting someone other than the pastor to conduct the training. If that is the case, the pastor, head deacon, or head deaconess would contact that person and plan around his/her schedule.

Try to arrive at the resort around 4:00 p.m. on a Friday (March-September ideally). The group should have enough time to get set up and finish supper by 7:00 p.m. Here is a suggested schedule of events for a weekend deacon and deaconess retreat.

THE SAMPLE S.D.A. CHURCH DEACON & DEACONESS RETREAT

The Nature House Christian Retreat
Anywhereville, AL
May 21-23, 2010

"Pure religion and undefiled before God and the Father is this, To visit the fatherless and widows in their affliction, and to keep himself [herself] unspotted from the world." James 1:27

Friday, May 21, 2010

4:00-6:00 p.m.	Arrival and Personal Preparation
6:00-7:15 p.m.	Supper

7:30-8:00 p.m.	Vesper
	   Song Service
	   Prayer
	   Special Music
	   Speaker- Deacon _____

8:00-8:05 p.m.	Break
8:05-8:30 p.m.	Group Exercise

8:30-8:55 p.m.	Prayer Session (Seek God's vision for Deacons and Deaconesses)
8:55-9:00 p.m.	Closing Remarks and Benediction

Sabbath, May 22, 2010

7:30-8:45 a.m.	Breakfast
9:15-10:30 a.m.	Sabbath School Song Service Prayer Special Music Lesson- Deaconess _____ Deacon _____
10:30-10:50 a.m.	Prayer Session (Seek God's vision for Deacons and Deaconesses)
10:50-11:00 a.m.	Break
11:00-12:00 p.m.	Presentation- Pastor/Presenter
12:00-12:05 p.m.	Break
12:05-1:05 p.m.	Group Exercise
1:30-2:45 p.m.	Lunch
3:00-5:00 p.m.	Hiking/Relaxation
5:00-5:30 p.m.	Group Exercise
5:30-5:45 p.m.	Prayer Session (Seek God's Power to fulfill His vision through us)

6:00-7:15 p.m.	Supper
7:30-8:00 p.m.	Vesper Song Service Prayer Special Music Speaker- Deacon _____
8:00-8:05 p.m.	Closing Remarks and Benediction
8:15-9:45 p.m.	Recreation

Sunday, May 23, 2010

8:30-9:45 a.m.	Breakfast
9:45-10:45 a.m.	Testimonies and Sharing
10:45-11:00 a.m.	Season of Prayer
11:00-12:00 p.m.	Cleaning and Packing
12:00 p.m.	Departure

To begin the work for the evening, have a vesper service with one of the deacons giving a vesper thought. Afterward, the pastor or guest presenter should state what he/she hopes that they will accomplish that weekend together—to seek God's vision for the deacon and deaconess board, develop vision and mission statements, and establish goals and objectives to be carried out upon returning home.

Divide the deacons and deaconesses into groups, consisting of no more than five in each group. Have a mix of deacons and deaconesses in each group. Each group will select a secretary and a facilitator. Everyone is given a Pleased and Troubled Worksheet on which to list the things they are pleased about and troubled about as a deacon or deaconess. As each person shares his/her list in their group, the secretary records it on a large master sheet and puts stars by those areas that are repeated. Then each person in the group will rank the pleased and troubled areas by putting a red dot by the areas that are most important to him/her, and a blue dot by the areas least important. Each group will turn in their big sheets to the pastor/presenter to be synthesized. Once they are synthesized, the goal is to continue to improve upon those areas in which they are pleased, and to implement strategies to address those areas in which they are troubled.

The next item scheduled for that evening is to have a twenty-five minute prayer session. The focus of the prayers is to thank God for what these officers are pleased about, seek direction in how to address their troubled areas, and to seek God's vision for them as deacons and deaconesses. If the prayer session goes beyond twenty-five minutes, that's okay. Prayer is the key that will bring about the results that these officers are seeking. After a few remarks by the pastor/presenter, and the benediction, the group is ready to settle in for the night.

Developing a Vision and Mission Statement

After breakfast Sabbath morning, a Sabbath school program should be conducted. At least one deacon and one deaconess should facilitate the lesson study. At the conclusion of the lesson, the group should have another prayer session to seek God's vision for them. After prayer and a ten minute break, the worship service follows. This consists of a presentation, ideally in PowerPoint that identifies the current problem of your local church and other Seventh-day Adventist churches. The problem is that the deacons and deaconesses of the Seventh-day Adventist church are under-utilized. They have been relegated to caring for the church facilities while the spiritual leadership responsibilities that were carried out by the deacons of the first century Christian church have been assigned to other departments established by the church.

The pastor/presenter should give examples from the Scriptures to show the biblical model that deacons and deaconesses of the twenty-first century should adopt. As the deacons and deaconesses listen to the presentation, they are to write on their Vision Worksheet the vision that God is revealing to them about their ministry. The pastor/presenter should also use the material in this book as a guide.

After the presentation, the deacons and deaconesses are to separate into their groups and share what they wrote on their Vision Worksheets, while the secretaries write it on a large master sheet. The same process is followed for this exercise as was followed with the Pleased and Troubled exercise. The synthesis of their worksheets will define the vision for their ministry. According to James M. Kouzes and Barry Z. Posner, "visions are statements of destination, of the ends of our labor; they are therefore future-oriented and are made real over different spans of time."[4] The following is an example of a vision statement for deacons and deaconesses:

VISION STATEMENT

The deacons and deaconesses of the Sample Seventh-day Adventist Church identified the following vision of themselves and their work: (1) being filled with the Holy Spirit, (2) being teachers and preachers, (3) being students of God's Word, (4) being soul winners, (5) being prayer warriors, (6) keeping order in the church, (7) coming together on one accord, (8) meeting once a month as a whole group–deacons and deaconesses together, (9) coming together to study and to be taught how to be effective, and (10) having seasons of prayer before Holy Communion.

---

[4]James M. Kouzes and Barry Z. Posner, *The Leadership Challenge* (San Francisco: Jossey-Bass, 2002), 130.

Dinner is served at the conclusion of the group session. Allow a couple of hours of leisure time after dinner for those who want to take a hike and/or relax.

After relaxing, the deacons and deaconesses are to meet in their groups again for another group exercise. This exercise involves the development of a mission statement and setting some goals and objectives to be accomplished in the near future. The same process is used as in the previous group sessions. The following is an example of a mission statement for deacons and deaconesses:

MISSION STATEMENT

The mission of the deacons and deaconesses of the Sample Seventh-day Adventist Church is to serve its members and community—especially those that are most vulnerable—by providing for their emergency physical, social, and spiritual needs, addressing relational problems in the church, and teaching and preaching God's Word through public and personal evangelism. We will lead people into a saving relationship with Jesus Christ and disciple newly baptized church members. We will visit, assess needs, and network with departments within the church and agencies in the community in order to accomplish our mission. We will be responsible for maintaining the upkeep of the church and its properties. We will engage in on-going personal development through prayer, the study of the Bible, the Spirit of Prophecy, and other relevant materials so that we might become better persons that are better equipped to glorify God and serve humanity.

Setting Goals and Objectives

The final task of this group exercise is for the deacons and deaconesses to set goals and objectives for them to carry out upon returning home. One example of a goal, in the context of the sample mission statement, is for the deacons and deaconesses to identify who are the "most vulnerable" individuals mentioned in the mission statement that they will serve. Define their needs. Develop ministries to meet those needs. Contact social service agencies in the community and invite their representatives to come and speak to the board of deacons and deaconesses; find out what services they offer to assist these individuals, and how the deacons and deaconesses can network with them. Finally, the deacons and deaconesses should identify both human and financial resources of the church that can assist in meeting the needs of these "most vulnerable" individuals. You should be able to obtain a list of all of the social services agencies in your community by asking any one of those agencies.

Whatever goals and objectives the deacons and deaconesses set at the retreat, they must be sure to establish a timeline for accomplishing them. The head deacon and head deaconesses must hold the members of their boards accountable for taking the necessary action steps to complete the tasks. Therefore, assignments should be made in this group exercise. The secretary of each group is to record the names of the deacons and deaconesses who agree to carry out assignments on an Action Steps Assignment Sheet. A date is set for the meeting when these officers will give their reports.

This group exercise concludes with a prayer session to seek God's power to fulfill His vision through the deacons and deaconesses. Supper is next, followed by a vesper service, closing remarks by the pastor/presenter, and an hour and a half of recreation before turning in for the night.

The final hours on Sunday morning begin with breakfast, followed by a time for testimonies and sharing, and conclude with a season of prayer. The pastor/presenter should have each of the deacons and deaconesses to fill out a Commitment Form (at the end of the chapter). Copies should be made so that they will have a copy as a reminder, and the head deacon/deaconess, and pastor will also have a copy as a reminder to pray for them.

These officers are now ready to depart from this mountain top experience to return to their church and community to serve. They are equipped with God's Spirit, a vision, a mission, goals, objectives, action steps, and the empowerment of their pastor and church family to accomplish their ministry.

DEACON AND DEACONESS COMMITMENT FORM

In as much as I have taken a critical look at the Biblical Roots of the office of Deacon and Deaconess, I am now willing to reshape my ministry so that it will fit the Biblical Model and be aligned with our Mission Statement. Therefore, I am making the following commitment:

Please check the appropriate line(s)

___ To spend at least one hour each day reading my Bible and praying for the infilling of the Holy Spirit and wisdom.

___ Become actively involved in visiting and nurturing the members of my church.

___ Use my influence to solve the problems that arise in the church that create dissatisfaction and murmuring among the membership.

___ To make sure that the church properties are maintained in such a way that they will always present a positive witness for God.

___ To be a team player, attend all of the scheduled meetings of my office, and faithfully carry out my assigned duties.

___ Become actively engaged in soul-winning by giving Bible studies, conducting cottage meetings in my home/community, passing out Bible tracts, or do some other form of evangelism in consultation with my Pastor.

___ Other:

Name _____

Address _____

Phone _____ Date _____

CHAPTER 24

Training Deacons and Deaconesses as Bible Workers

The deacons and deaconesses of the first century Christian church taught God's Word and brought converts into the church. The deacon Philip not only conducted evangelistic meetings, but he also conducted one-on-one Bible studies (Acts 8:5-8, 26-40; 21:8). Priscilla along with her husband Aquila gave Bible studies to Apollos, "an eloquent man, and mighty in the scriptures" (Acts 18:24-28). Therefore, it should be expected that the deacons and deaconesses of the twenty-first century teach God's Word and win converts to the church. According to the material presented in chapter 8 of this book, deacons and deaconesses are to serve in the role of teachers of God's Word. The advantage of deacons and deaconesses serving as Bible workers over the church hiring Bible workers who are not members of the church is the deacons and deaconesses will remain at the church to nurture the people that join the church through their teaching. Usually hired Bible workers are used to work in an evangelistic meeting conducted by the church. When the meeting is over, they will leave. Because the people who join the church get attached to the Bible worker who studies with them, if the worker leaves, the possibility is that they will leave eventually.

To equip deacons and deaconesses to serve as Bible workers of the church, the pastor should help facilitate them being properly trained. He may choose to train them himself or have someone who is currently serving or has previously served as a Bible worker to train them. There are several soul-winning manuals and other witnessing material on the market that provide instructions on how to give Bible studies. There is also a plethora of Bible study guides and lessons from which to choose from.

One source, although it is dated it is practical, is the *New Testament Witnessing* by Elden K. Walter. Walter emphasizes the power of the personal testimony. Referring to Revelation 12:11, "And they overcame him [Satan] by the blood of the Lamb and the word of their testimony," he says, "Two things are mentioned in this verse of scripture as a means of conquering power: 1) the blood of the Lamb which purchased our salvation on Calvary and without which we would be hopeless, 2) another source of power which is rarely recognized or discussed, **the word of their testimony.**"[5]

Writing Your Personal Testimony

For many people, making the initial contact is the most fearful part of the process of giving Bible studies. Some are afraid of talking to people who are struggling with lifestyles that they know nothing about, such as drugs or prostitution. If you have this fear, it is important for you to understand that people who are struggling with these issues are experiencing the same emotions as you experienced when you were struggling with your issues. The issues may be different, the way people deal with their emotions is different, but the emotions are the same. Therefore, when trying to witness to or enroll people in Bible studies, it is important that you use your personal testimony to make an emotional connection with them. All sinners without Christ are empty, lonely, miserable, hopeless, sad, etc. Everyone has experienced these emotions regardless of his/her lifestyle. Drug addicts use drugs to cope with these emotions. Prostitutes use sex and maybe drugs also. Other people use food, people, material possessions, education, etc. Bible workers are to help all people that they come in contact with to understand that only Jesus can heal their damaged emotions and fill the void in their lives caused by sin.

Here is an example of a personal testimony. It is divided into four sections.

PERSONAL TESTIMONY (3-4 minutes)

My Life Before I Met Christ:

I was empty, lonely, and miserable. I did everything I knew to do to

---

[5]Elden K. Walter, *New Testament Witnessing*, 3rd ed. (Richardson, TX: Elden K. Walter, 1972), 31.

try to fill the void in my life. I tried losing myself in the crowd to forget about who I was because I didn't like who I was.

How I Realized I Needed Christ:

When everything I tried didn't work; when the mornings after the late night parties left me feeling more miserable and less fulfilled; when I recognized that my so-called friends were just using me; and when I was dying inside and feeling hopeless because of unemployment and discouragement, I realized that I needed Christ.

How I Became a Christian:

I read a book written by an entertainer that I admired. Surprisingly, he talked about God and faith. This caused me to reflect on my Christian up-bringing, so I decided to give God another try. I started praying, reading my Bible, and listening to preaching on the radio. I saw God answering my prayers. I saw my life changing.

The Difference Christ has Made in My Life:

Now that I have Christ in my life, I am complete. The void has been filled. I have peace, joy, and hope. The search is over. I no longer have to live a sinful life trying to find fulfillment. Jesus has set me free!

Deacons and deaconesses should write out their personal testimony as they prepare to accept the challenge of serving as Bible workers for their church. In addition to the personal testimony, Walter suggests that the Gospel Presentation be used as a witnessing tool. This is the outline of the presentation.

The Gospel Presentation

I. **Introduction**
   A. Their secular life
   B. Their church life
   C. Our Testimony—Church or Personal
   D. The Two Questions:

        1. Have you come to the place in your spiritual life where if you were to die tonight you would know for certain that you would have eternal life?

        2. Suppose that you were to die tonight and when you meet God, if He were to ask, "Why should you have eternal life in heaven? What would you say?

II.   The Gospel

  A. Grace

    1. Eternal life is a gift. [Eph 2:8-9]

    2. We can't earn or deserve it. [Titus 3:5]

  B. Man

    1. We are sinners. [Rom 3:23]

    2. We cannot save ourselves.

  C. God

    1. Is merciful—does not want to punish us. [Rom 6:23]

    2. Is just, therefore must punish sin.

  D. Christ

    1. The infinite God-man [John 3:16]

    2. God's punishment for sin was placed on Him. [1 Pet 2:24]

  E. Faith

    1. By faith that trusts Christ alone.

    2. Distinguish from intellectual, temporal faith. [John 3:36]

  F. Acceptance

    1. Receiving the gift of Eternal Life. [1 John 5:13]

    2. Our Covenant (agreement) with God.

III.   The New Life

  A. Sins forgiven

  B. New Creation

  C. Sons and daughters of God

  D. Winning Life

  E. Eternal Life

IV.   **The Commitment**
A. Qualifying Question—Do you see what Christ wants to do for you?
B. Commitment Question—Do you want to receive the gift of Eternal Life that Christ left heaven and died on the cross to give you?
C. Clarification of Commitment
1. Transferring trust from self to Christ.
2. Christ must be Lord as well as Saviour.
D. Prayer of Commitment
If this is really what you want, we can go to the Lord in prayer. I can lead us in prayer and we will tell Him what you have told me just now. Prayer ...
E. Assurance
1. [Read *Steps to Christ*]
2. Fix in the mind the texts of assurance. [2 Cor 5:17; John 1:12; 1 John 3:2]

V.   **Welcome to the Family of God!**[6]

What is encouraging about the Gospel Presentation is that the Bible worker takes the person through the essential steps of receiving salvation, gives him/her hope, and accepts the person as a member of the family of God in that one encounter. I also recommend that the Bible worker give him/her the book *Steps to Christ* by Ellen G. White to read, and establish a time to meet with the person the following week to discuss chapter 1. Use this book as a study tool before introducing doctrinal lessons. Another option is to use easy Christ-centered Bible study guides instead of *Steps to Christ*, followed by advanced doctrinal lessons that are also Christ-centered. I offer the following Bible study guides as an example. The entire course contains twenty-four lessons (8 Regular, 8 Advanced 1, and 8 Advanced 2). You may contact the author of this book if you are interested in obtaining a set of these lessons.

_____

[6]Ibid., 49.

Jesus Is The Answer Bible Study Course
(Regular) Lesson 1

HOW DID WE GET GOD'S SPOKEN
WORD, THE BIBLE?

The Bible is a collection of 66 books which was written over a period of 1,500 years. Nearly 40 men were involved in writing the Bible. It is divided into two testaments—the Old Testament and the New Testament. The Old Testament contains 39 books and the New Testament contains 27. The Bible is God's love letter to us. The more we read it, the more we see how much God loves us.

Directions: These statements are either TRUE or FALSE. Read the Bible texts at the end of each statement, then circle TRUE or FALSE. PRAY FIRST!

1. The men who wrote the Bible (prophecy) wrote and spoke from their own will and imagination (2 Peter 1:21).   **TRUE-FALSE**
2. The New Testament is the only part of the Bible that God inspired to be written (2 Timothy 3:16-17).   **TRUE-FALSE**
3. The Bible was written to give us hope (Romans 15:4).
    TRUE-FALSE
4. We have to study the Bible if we are to understand it correctly (2 Timothy 2:15).   **TRUE-FALSE**
5. JESUS IS THE ANSWER. The Scriptures testify that He is the one that we must go to to receive eternal life (John 5:39-40).
    TRUE-FALSE

Name _____ Address _____

City _____ State_____ Zip_____ Phone _____

Date _____

Jesus Is The Answer Bible Study Course
(Advanced 1) Lesson 9

WHAT WILL HAPPEN WHEN JESUS COMES?

Most of the signs and Bible prophecies pointing to the second coming of Jesus have been fulfilled. The heavenly court has been in session for over a century now. The next event to occur is the coming of the Lord. I want to be ready, what about you?

Directions: These statements are either TRUE or FALSE. Read the Bible texts at the end of each statement, then circle TRUE or FALSE. PRAY FIRST!

1. Before Jesus left to go to heaven, He did not say anything about returning to this earth. (John 14:1-3) **TRUE-FALSE**
2. When Jesus comes, He is not coming secretly. Everybody will know that He has come. (Matthew 24:26-27, 30; Revelation 1:7) **TRUE-FALSE**
3. When Jesus comes, He is going to be real quiet and sneak the good people to heaven and leave the wicked on earth to "party hardy." (2 Peter 3:10; 2 Thessalonians 1:7-9) **TRUE-FALSE**
4. When Jesus comes, the first resurrection will occur. The righteous dead will be raised out of their graves. (1 Thessalonians 4:16) **TRUE-FALSE**
5. JESUS IS THE ANSWER. After He resurrects the righteous dead from their graves, He will catch the righteous living up in the air with them, and take them all back to heaven with Him. (1 Thessalonians 4:17) **TRUE-FALSE**

Name_____ Address _____

City_____ State _____ Zip _____ Phone _____

Date_____

Jesus Is The Answer Bible Study Course
(Advanced 2) Lesson 17

HOW CAN I POSTPONE MY FUNERAL?

Recently the area of diet has been studied with regards to cancer and other deadly diseases. Medical research reveals that there is a direct relationship between diet and disease. God has much to say about the way we should eat. Let us learn what He has to say!

Directions: These statements are either TRUE or FALSE. Read the Bible texts at the end of each statement, then circle TRUE or FALSE. PRAY FIRST!

1. God is not concerned about whether or not we have healthy bodies. (3 John 2)   **TRUE-FALSE**
2. The foods that we eat and the way that we treat our bodies play a very important part in our Christian experience. (I Corinthians 10:31; 6:19-20; 3:16-17)   **TRUE-FALSE**
3. The original diet that God gave to man consisted of: "Herb bearing seed"—grains; and "Fruit of a tree yielding seed"—fruits and nuts. (Genesis 1:29)   **TRUE-FALSE**
4. God said, "If an animal or fish tastes good, eat it." (Leviticus 11:1-31)   **TRUE-FALSE**
5. It's okay if we eat barbeque pig or swine meat under the trees at the park. (Isaiah 66:15-17)   **TRUE-FALSE**
6. God also warns us against using alcoholic beverages and everything that impairs our health or causes our death, such as tobacco and drugs. (Proverbs 20:1; 23:29-32)   **TRUE-FALSE**
7. JESUS IS THE ANSWER. He set an example for us. Although He drank unfermented wine/grape juice, He refused to take drugs. (Matthew 27:33-34)   **TRUE-FALSE**

Name_____ Address _____

City_____ State____ Zip _____ Phone _____

Date_____

Watching for Prospects

We are admonished by Ellen G. White that "the gospel invitation is to be given to rich and poor, the high and the low, and we must devise means for carrying the truth into new places, and to all classes of people."[7] White also reminded us that "Christ method alone will give true success in reaching the people. The Saviour mingled with men as one who desired their good. He showed His sympathy for them, ministered to their needs, and won their confidence. Then He bade them, `Follow Me.'"[8]

WHO ARE THE PROSPECTS?

1. Health conscious people whom you frequently see at vegetarian restaurants, walking tracks, and health spas
2. People who visit SDA churches
3. Relatives of SDAs
4. People who have received treatment at SDA medical facilities
5. Neighbors of SDAs
6. People helped by SDA Community Services Centers
7. Un-churched people who are searching for a better life
8. Members of other faiths who are dissatisfied with their church
9. Customers of SDA owned and operated businesses
10. Employees of SDA owned and operated businesses
11. Non-SDA employers of SDAs
12. Schoolmates of SDA youth attending public schools
13. Non-SDA youth attending SDA schools
14. Non-SDA parents of youth attending SDA schools
15. Co-workers of SDAs
16. Honest-hearted ministers of other faiths
17. People who have purchased books from SDA Literature Evangelists

---

[7]Ellen White, *Evangelism*, 552.

[8]Ellen White, *The Ministry of Healing*, 143.

HOW TO WITNESS TO PROSPECTS?

1. Be a silent witness by your own life-style
2. Be consistent in actions and words
3. Respect their opinions; seek their advice in areas where they are knowledgeable
4. Agree with them whenever you can without compromising godly principles
5. Be an active listener
6. Share your personal testimony when it relates to troubles and important issues that they are facing
7. Give them literature on issues of interest to them (healthful living; vegetarian recipes; prophecies relating to current events; etc.)
8. Invite them to church programs that address topics of interest to them
9. Be a friend
10. Look for opportunities to help
11. Accept invitations from them to attend programs of mutual interest
12. Invite them to church sponsored social events
13. Invite them to a small group cottage meeting
14. Study the Bible with them
15. Invite them to church sponsored evangelistic meetings

Finally, I recommend that the deacons and deaconesses who are willing to accept the challenge to become Bible workers for their churches use the Community Prayer Request approach in conjunction with the Gospel Presentation. The following is a canvass for this approach:

COMMUNITY PRAYER REQUEST FORM

Good evening! My name is _____ from the Sample Community Prayer Ministry. We are praying for you and the residents of our community. Is there anything in particular that you would like for us to pray about concerning you or your family?

Prayer Request_____
_____
_____

We have special prayer meetings on Wednesdays at 12:00 noon and 6:00 p.m. We will be praying for your situation. To help us to know how to pray for your spiritual walk with God, do you mind if I ask you two questions? ____ Yes No ____

1. Have you come to the place in your spiritual life where if you were to die tonight you would know for certain that you would have eternal life? ____ Yes No ____
2. Suppose that you were to die tonight and when you meet God, if He were to ask, "Why should you have eternal life in heaven? What would you say?

(Proceed to give the Gospel Presentation. Use your personal testimony where appropriate. Leave them a *Steps to Christ*, or lessons 1 and 2 of the Jesus is the Answer Bible Study Course.)

What day next week can I come by to see how God is answering your prayer request, and to discuss chapter 1 of the book/Bible lessons with you? _____. May I pray with you now? ____ Yes No ____   (Prayer)

See you next _____ at ____ o'clock. Have a blessed day!

Name _____ Address_____

City _____State_____ Zip_____ Phone _____

Date _____

Conclusion

A strategy for developing and implementing a twenty-first century ministry for deacons and deaconesses that reflects the first century model requires educating the church membership concerning the biblical role of deacons and deaconesses. The Book of Acts provides the theological framework for this. The first century Christian church is the model that provides the necessary instructions. Its members:

> . . . continued stedfastly in the apostles' doctrine and fellowship, and in breaking of bread, and in prayers. And they, continuing daily with one accord in the temple, and breaking bread from house to house, did eat their meat with gladness and singleness of heart, praising God, and having favour with all the people. And the Lord added to the church daily such as should be saved (Acts 2:42, 46, and 47).

As the members apply these principles to their lives—prayer, study and obey God's Word, unity, fellowship, and attend church faithfully—they will become more acceptant to change. The series of sermons will create a desire to return to the biblical model.

The training retreat will give the deacons and deaconesses a vision, a mission, and a sense of direction. Training them to serve as Bible workers will equip them to perform a broader ministry that will better meet the needs of the church and community. The result will be as it was in the first century Christian church: "The Lord added to the church daily such as should be saved" (Acts 2:47).

Summary

The theology of ministry for deacons and deaconesses is established upon the servant model foundation that was demonstrated in the life of Jesus. Jesus came into the world to minister (διακονῆσαι) and not to be ministered unto (διακονηθῆναι) (Matt 20:28). These two Greek words come from the root word διακονέω which is derived from the word διάκονος (deacon)—masculine and feminine. Therefore, the act of ministering or serving is inherent in the name deacon and deaconess, and defines the nature of the office.

The deacons that served the first century Christian church solved problems that arose in the church, took care of the needs of the poor, and taught the Word of God. They were ordained to carry out their responsibilities.

The deaconesses that served the first century Christian church took care of the poor and sick among the females, taught the Word of God, assisted women at baptisms, greeted the women entering the church, and directed them to their seats. During the first five centuries, deaconesses were also ordained to carry out their responsibilities.

Very little is recorded about the work of deacons and deaconesses in the early Seventh-day Adventist church. It is recorded that it was the responsibility of the deacons to provide unfermented grape juice for Holy Communion, and collect the tithe. In the large churches, the deacons turned the tithe over to the church treasurer. However, in the small churches, a deacon served as the treasurer. They were ordained just as their first century counterparts.

The deaconesses that served the early Seventh-day Adventist church visited the sick, looked after the young, ministered to the necessities of the poor, and listened to the women who had troubles that they wanted to share. They were also ordained to carry out their responsibilities. However, beginning in 1914 they were no longer ordained. In 1990 the ordination service for deaconesses was replaced with an induction service. However, at the recently held 59th General Conference Session the delegates voted that deaconesses should be ordained along with deacons.

Several underlying factors, which are based upon the tradition and culture of the Seventh-day Adventist church, have created a systemic problem for its deacons and deaconesses. These factors are (1) very little was recorded about the work of deacons and deaconesses during the early history of the Seventh-day Adventist church, (2) other departments were established that eventually supplanted the role and function of deacons and deaconesses, (3) deacons and deaconesses have been marginalized and relegated to caring for the church facilities, collecting tithes and offerings, and serving during Holy Communion and baptism, and (4) the church discontinued the ordination of deaconesses for almost a century but is in continual discussion about the ordination of female elders and female pastors. Due to these underlying factors, deacons and deaconesses of the Seventh-day Adventist church find it difficult to follow the biblical model for their ministry. However, by becoming aware of the problem and being willing to embrace recommendations for change, the cycle can be broken. The recommendations are (1) local churches elect people who meet the biblical qualifications for deacons and deaconesses so that they will have the spiritual gifts and commitment to fulfill the responsibilities required of that office, (2) utilize deacons and deaconesses' leadership skills by electing them to serve as leaders of other departments in the church, (3) assign deacons and deaconesses along with the elders to other departments to serve as liaisons for the pastor, (4) utilize deacons and deaconesses along with the elders to visit the members, facilitate mid-week prayer meetings, resolve conflicts in the church, and give Bible studies, (5) provide deacons and deaconesses sufficient resources to care for the sick and needy, and (6) empower them to serve as physical plant managers.

Now that the Seventh-day Adventist church has taken action to ordain deaconesses again, it is imperative that it provides training for them beyond what has been traditionally given. I recommend to the Seventh-day Adventist church at large that it (1) restore deacons and deaconesses to their biblically defined roles as spiritual leaders of the church, (2) invite pastors and elders to attend deacons and deaconesses training sessions so that they can better understand the role of these officers and the value that they have to contribute to the work, (3) put as much emphasis on the development of deacons and deaconesses as is put on the development of other church officers, (4) sponsor retreats and summits for them, (5) produce a handbook and a quarterly magazine for them, and (6) train the deacons and deaconesses of newly organized churches so that the current trends will not continue to be perpetuated. When dignity is restored to the office of deaconess, the tension over the ordination of female elders and pastors will be reduced. Women that are called of God to minister will count it a privilege to serve in the office of deaconess.

The call to serve as a deacon or deaconess is a spiritual calling. This can be readily seen by observing the spiritual qualifications required of those who were called to serve in this office in the first century Christian church. The call to wait on tables was, in fact, a call to solve relational problems that arose in the church. Therefore, deacons and deaconesses are called to serve as spiritual counselors, conflict managers, and social workers; as well as Bible workers and evangelists.

There are wider implications that can be drawn from the ministry of deacons and deaconesses for the church at large. Since the deacon and deaconess symbolize the work of the church, every church member is a deacon or deaconess although he or she may not bear the title. Jesus is the "Deacon" par excellence, and calls everyone who becomes a member of His church to a ministry of service.

The New Testament reveals little information about the existence of female deacons or deaconesses and the role that they played in the first century Christian church. In that the Greek word διάκονος can be translated in various ways, the way in which it is translated to describe Phoebe's position (Rom 16:1-2) depends upon the presupposition of the translator. Similar ambivalence surrounds the interpretation of the Greek word for "wives" in 1 Tim 3:11 KJV, whether it should be translated so that the text means deacons' wives or women deacons/deaconesses. Since the possessive form of διάκονος is not present in this text, the most favorable translation is "women." Therefore, Paul was addressing women deacons or deaconesses, not the wives of deacons.

There is evidence to substantiate the fact that female deacons or deaconesses existed during the early centuries. The *Didascalia Apostolorum* (third century), the *Apostolic Constitutions* (late fourth century), inscriptions written on the tombstones of female deacons or deaconesses during the fourth through the seventh centuries, and current literature from both Protestant and Catholic writers provide this evidence.

There are four important roles in which deacons and deaconesses are to function: the role of teachers of God's Word, care givers to the sick and needy, conflict managers, and physical plant managers. In some denominations, the deacon board serves as business managers instead of physical plant managers. This has caused a shift in focus from serving the members to running the church.

There are many other responsibilities that deacons and deaconesses are to carry out. They are to welcome the members and visitors as they enter the church and assist them find seats when necessary. They are to visit the members, minister to the bereaved, assist at funerals, fellowship dinners, baptismal and Holy Communion services, and minister to members by serving on the telephone committee. They are to attend all of the services of the church and participate in various capacities as needed. Deacons are to collect tithes and offerings and assist the treasurer in counting the funds.

The ministry of deacons and deaconesses is multi-faceted. These officers are gifted and chosen by God. It is my earnest prayer that the church will restore them to their biblical role as spiritual leaders of the church, train, equip, and empower them to provide a ministry in the twenty-first century that reflects the ministry of the deacons and deaconesses of the first century Christian church.

BIBLIOGRAPHY

"Acts." *Seventh-day Adventist Bible Commentary.* Edited by Francis D. Nichol. 1956. Reprint, Washington, DC: Review and Herald Publishing Assn., 1980. 6:187-244.

Adventist Review. "Sixth Business Meeting Proceedings: Church Manual Only." www.adventistreview.org/article.php?id=3510 (accessed July 5, 2010).

Agan, Clarence DeWitt "Jimmy," III. "Deacons, Deaconesses, and Denominational Discussions: Romans 16:1 as a Test Case." *Presbyterion* 34, no. 2 (Fall 2008): 93-108.

Bancroft, Jane Marie. *Deaconesses in Europe and Their Lessons for America.* 1890. Reprint, Charleston, SC: BiblioBazaar, LLC, 2008.

Barksdale, Annie. *The Holy Spirit.* Stamford, CT: Annie Barksdale, 2002.

Barnett, James Monroe. *The Diaconate—A Full and Equal Order: A Comprehensive and Critical Study of Origin, Development, and Decline of the Diaconate in the Context of the Church's Total Ministry and a Proposal for Renewal.* New York: Seabury Press, 1981.

Becker, Penny Edgell. *Congregations in Conflict: Cultural Models of Local Religious Life.* New York: Cambridge University Press, 1999.

Brill, Naomi I. *Working with People: The Helping Process.* 2nd ed. New York: J. B. Lippincott Company, 1978.

Brown, Rosalind. *Being a Deacon Today.* Harrisburg, PA: Morehouse Publishing, 2005

Burnett, John Franklin. *The Church the Pillar and Ground of the Truth.* 1917. Reprint, Charleston, SC: BiblioLife, 2009.

Burns, Thomas R. *Basic Counseling for Deacons: A Guide for Interviewing.* Rio Rancho, NM: Thomas Burns, 2008.

"Called the Multitude." *Seventh-day Adventist Bible Commentary*. Edited by Francis D. Nichol. 1956. Reprint, Washington, DC: Review and Herald Publishing Assn., 1980. 6:189.

Catoe, Kenneth D. "Equipping Deacons for Ministry." D.Min. dissertation, Drew University, 1989.

Chadwick, Owen. *The Early Reformation on the Continent*. New York: Oxford University Press, 2001.

Church of England. *For Such a Time as This: A Renewed Diaconate in the Church of England*. London: Church House Publishing, 2001.

Collins, Jim. *Good to Great*. New York: HarperCollins Publishers, Inc., 2001.

Collins, John N. *Deacons and the Church: Making Connections Between Old and New*. Harrisburg, PA: Morehouse Publishing, 2002.

Cress, James A. *You Can Keep Them If You Care: Helping New Members Stay on Board*. Silver Spring, MD: The Ministerial Association General Conference of Seventh-day Adventists, 2000.

Cullinan, Edmond. "Women and the Diaconate." *Worship* 70, no. 3 (May 1996): 260-266.

Davis, Diana. *Deacon Wives: Fresh Ideas to Encourage Your Husband and the Church*. Nashville: B & H Publishing Group, 2009.

"The Deaconate." *Seventh-day Adventist Bible Commentary*. Edited by Francis D. Nichol. 1956. Reprint, Washington, DC: Review and Herald Publishing Assn., 1980. 6:25-26.

Deweese, Charles W. *The Emerging Role of Deacons*. Nashville: Broadman Press, 1979.

_____. *Women Deacons and Deaconesses: 400 Years of Baptist Service*. Macon, GA: Mercer University Press, 2005.

Dockery, David S. "Acts 6-12: The Christian Mission Beyond Jerusalem." *Review and Expositor* 87 (Summer 1990): 423-437.

Earle, Alice Morse. *Sabbath in Puritan New England.* 7th ed. Teddington, Middlesex, England: The Echo Library, 2007.

Echlin, Edward P. *The Deacon in the Church: Past Time and Future.* Staten Island, NY: Alba House, 1971.

Eisen, Ute E. *Women Officeholders in Early Christianity: Epigraphical and Literary Studies.* Collegeville, MN: Liturgical Press, 2000.

Ellis, Janice Rider, and Celia Love Hartley. *Nursing in Today's World: Trends, Issues and Management.* 8th ed. Philadelphia, PA: Lippincott Williams and Wilkins, 2004.

"Evangelical." http://wordnetweb.princeton.edu/perl/webwn?s =evangelical (accessed February 19, 2009).

"Faith." *Seventh-day Adventist Bible Commentary.* Edited by Francis D. Nichol. 1956. Reprint, Washington, DC: Review and Herald Publishing Assn., 1980. 7:299-300.

Finley, Ernestine, and Mark Finley. *Light Your World for God.* Fallbrook, CA: Hart Books, 2002.

Fletcher, Anne M. *Sober for Good: New Solutions for Drinking Problems— Advice from Those Who Have Succeeded.* New York: Houghton Mifflin Company, 2001.

Foshee, Howard B. *Now That You're a Deacon.* Nashville: Broadman Press, 1975.

Freed John. "Liturgical Worship: Assets and Liabilities of the Formal Model." The Freed School Blog, entry posted July 25, 2006. http://freedschool.blogspot.com/2006_07_01_archive.html (accessed February 19, 2009).

Gaillardetz, Richard R. *The Church in the Making: Lumen Gentium, Christus Dominus, Orientalium Ecclesiarum.* Mahwah, NJ: Paulist Press, 2006.

General Conference of Seventh-day Adventists. "History of Adventist Community Services International." http://www .sabbathschoolpersonalministries.org/article.php?id=49 (accessed May 14, 2009).

_____. *Manual for Church Officers.* Washington, DC: Ministerial Assn., 1978.

_____. *Minister's Manual.* Silver Spring, MD: Ministerial Assn., 1992.

_____. "Personal Ministries." http://www .sabbathschoolpersonalministries.org/article.php?id=3 (accessed May 17, 2009).

_____. *Seventh-day Adventist Church Manual.* Hagerstown, MD: Review and Herald Publishing Assn., 2005.

Glasscock, Ed. "'The Husband of One Wife' Requirement in 1 Timothy 3:2." *Bibliotheca Sacra* 140 (July-September 1983): 244-258.

"Grave." *Seventh-day Adventist Bible Commentary.* Edited by Francis D. Nichol. 1956. Reprint, Washington, DC: Review and Herald Publishing Assn., 1980. 7:299.

Gray, Don, and Marjorie Gray. *You Are My Witness: Sharing Jesus in the 21st Century.* Keene, TX: Seminars Unlimited, 2003.

Green, Jay P., Sr., gen. ed. and trans. *The Interlinear Bible: Hebrew-Greek-English.* 2nd ed. Peabody, MA: Hendrickson Publishers, 1986.

Green, Michael. *Evangelism in the Early Church.* Grand Rapids, MI: Wm. B. Eerdmans Publishing, 1970.

Greenleaf, Robert K. *Servant Leadership: A Journey into the Nature of Legitimate Power and Greatness.* 1977. Reprint. Mahwah, NJ: Paulist Press, 2002.

Groh, Shirley A. "The Role of Deaconess Through History," December 1955. http://www .wlsessays.net/files/GrohRole .pdf (accessed October 13, 2008).

Hastings, James, ed. *A Dictionary of the Bible.* Vol. 3, pt. 2. Honolulu: University Press of the Pacific, 2004.

Hiebert, D. Edmond. "Behind the Word 'Deacon': A New Testament Study." *Bibliotheca Sacra* 140 (April-June 1983): 151-162.

Huels, John M. "Special Questions on the Diaconate." *Liturgical Ministry* 13 (Winter 2004): 1-9.

Johnson, Earl S. *The Presbyterian Deacon: An Essential Guide.* Louisville, KY: Geneva Press, 2002.

Karambai, Sebastian S. *Ministers and Ministries in the Local Church: A Comprehensive Guide to Ecclesiastical Norms.* Bandra, Mumbai, India: The Bombay Saint Paul Society, 2005.

Koranteng-Pipim, Samuel. *Must We Be Silent?.* Ann Arbor, MI: Berean Books, 2001.

Kouzes, James M., and Barry Z. Posner. *The Leadership Challenge.* San Francisco: Jossey-Bass, 2002.

Lewis, Robert M. "The 'Women' of 1 Timothy 3:11." *Bibliotheca Sacra* 136 (April-June 1979): 167-175.

Madigan, Kevin, and Carolyn Osiek, eds. and trans. *Ordained Women in the Early Church: A Documentary History.* Baltimore, MD: The John Hopkins University Press, 2005.

Merkle, Benjamin L. *40 Questions about Elders and Deacons.* Grands Rapids, MI: Kregel Publications, 2008.

Moody, Dwight A. *Heaven for a Dime: Memoir of a Small Town Preacher.* Lincoln, NE: Winter's Showcase, 2002.

Moulton, Harold, ed. *The Analytical Greek Lexicon.* Rev. ed. Grand Rapids, MI: Zondervan Publishing House, 1978. S.v. "διάκονος."

Naylor, Robert E. *The Baptist Deacon.* Nashville: Broadman Press, 1955.

"New Commandment." *Seventh-day Adventist Bible Commentary.* Edited by Francis D. Nichol. 1956. Reprint, Washington, DC: Review and Herald Publishing Assn., 1980. 5:1031-1032.

216   **Bibliography**

Nichols, Harold. *The Work of the Deacon and Deaconess.* Valley Forge, PA: Judson Press, 1964.

Norman, R. Steven, III. *Funeral Planning Made Simple*, 4th ed. Nashville: GESS Books International, 1995.

Oltman, Adele. *Sacred Mission, Worldly Ambition: Black Christian Nationalism in the Age of Jim Crow.* Athens, GA: University of Georgia Press, 2008.

"One Wife." *Seventh-day Adventist Bible Commentary.* Edited by Francis D. Nichol. 1956. Reprint, Washington, DC: Review and Herald Publishing Assn., 1980. 7:298.

Pierce, Ronald W., and Rebecca Merrill Groothuis, gen. eds. *Discovering Biblical Equality: Complementarity without Hierarchy.* 2nd ed. Contributing Editor Gordon D. Fee. Downers Grove, IL: InterVarsity Press, 2005.

Pitts, Bill. "Women, Ministry, and Identity: Establishing Female Deacons at First Baptist Church, Waco, Texas." *Baptist History and Heritage* 42, no. 1 (Winter 2007): 71-84.

Riley, Maurice. *The Deaconess: Walking in the Newness of Life.* 2nd ed. Newark, NJ: Christian Associates Publications, 1993.

Robinson, Anthony B., and Robert W. Wall. *Called to be Church: The Book of Acts for a New Day.* Grand Rapids, MI: Wm. B. Eerdmans Publishing, 2006.

Robinson, Cecilia. *The Ministry of Deaconesses.* 1898. Reprint, Charleston, SC: BiblioBazaar, LLC, 2008.

Rost, Joseph C. *Leadership for the Twenty-First Century.* 1991. Reprint, Westport, CT: Praeger Publishers, 1993.

Schaff, Philip. *Apostolic Christianity (A.D. 1-100). Vol. 1 of History of the Christian Church.* 1910. Reprint, Grand Rapids, MI: Wm. B. Eerdmans Publishing, 1985.

_____. *Nicene and Post-Nicene Christianity (A.D. 311-600). Vol. 3 of History of the Christian Church.* 1910. Reprint, Grand Rapids, MI: Wm. B. Eerdmans Publishing, 1985.

"Servant." *Seventh-day Adventist Bible Commentary*. Edited by Francis D. Nichol. 1956. Reprint, Washington, DC: Review and Herald Publishing Assn., 1980. 6:649.

Speer, William. *God's Rule for Christian Giving: A Practical Essay on the Source of Christian Economy*. 1923. Reprint, Charleston, SC: BiblioLife, 2009.

Straub, Gary, and James Trader, II. *Your Calling as a Deacon*. St. Louis, MO: Chalice Press, 2005.

"Usher Ministry Description." http://plusline.org/article.php?id=320 (accessed November 22, 2010).

Vine, W. E. *Expository Dictionary of New Testament Words*. Grand Rapids, MI: Zondervan Publishing House, 1952. S.v.v. "Doubletongued," "Mystery."

Vyhmeister, Nancy J. "Deaconesses in the Church." *Ministry*, September 2008, 22-27.

_____. "Deaconesses in History and in the Seventh-day Adventist Church." *Andrews University Seminary Studies* 43, no. 1 (2005): 133-158.

_____. "The Ministry of the Deaconess Through History." *Ministry*, July 2008, 17-20.

Walter, Elden K. *New Testament Witnessing*. 3rd ed. Richardson, TX: Elden K. Walter, 1972.

"Way of God." *Seventh-day Adventist Bible Commentary*. Edited by Francis D. Nichol. 1956. Reprint, Washington, DC: Review and Herald Publishing Assn., 1980. 6:369.

Webb, Henry. *Deacons: Servant Models in the Church*. Nashville: Convention Press, 1980.

_____. *Equipping Deacons in Church Growth Skills*. Nashville: Convention Press, 1982.

Wheatley, Margaret J. *Leadership and the New Science: Discovering Order in a Chaotic World*. San Francisco: Berrett-Koehler Publishers, 1999.

White, Ellen G. *Ellen G. White Writings.* Complete Published Edition 2005. S.v.v. "deacons," "deaconesses." CD-ROM. Silver Spring, MD: Ellen G. White Estate, 2006.

_____. *The Acts of the Apostles.* Boise, ID: Pacific Press, 1911.

_____. *The Desire of Ages.* 1898. Reprint, Mountain View, CA: Pacific Press, 1940.

_____. *Evangelism.* 1946. Reprint, Hagerstown, MD: Review and Herald Publishing Assn., 1970.

_____. *The Ministry of Healing.* 1905. Reprint, Nampa, ID: Pacific Press, 1942.

_____. *Steps to Christ.* 1892. Reprint, Hagerstown, MD: Review and Herald Publishing Assn., 1977.

_____. *The Story of Redemption.* 1947. Reprint, Hagerstown, MD: Review and Herald Publishing Assn., 1980.

_____. *Testimonies for the Church.* 9 vols. Boise, ID: Pacific Press, 1948.

White, Vincent E., Sr. *Problem Solvers and Soul Winners: A Handbook for Deacons and Deaconesses.* Huntsville, AL: AVA's Book Publishers, 1999.

Wijngaards, John. "The History of Women Deacons," http://www.womenpriests.org/traditio/deac_his.asp (accessed October 14, 2008).

"Wine." *Seventh-day Adventist Bible Commentary.* Edited by Francis D. Nichol. 1956. Reprint, Washington, DC: Review and Herald Publishing Assn., 1980. 7:299.

Wordworth, Christopher. *The New Testament of Our Lord and Saviour Jesus Christ.* 1923. Reprint, Charleston, SC: BiblioLife, LLC, 2009.

Xavier, Eurico Tadeu. "Deacons Take Care of Almost Everything." Translated by Antonio A. Rios. *Elder's Digest* 10, January-March 2004, 6-7.

Index of Subjects

Index of Scripture Texts

Index of Spirit of Prophecy Writings

Dr. Vincent E. White, Sr. is available to conduct Deacon and Deaconess Week-end Training Seminars; and also to speak at special occasions involving Deacons and Deaconesses. For more information, you may contact him at avasbp@att.net.

To purchase additional copies of this book—*The Twenty-First Century Deacon and Deaconess: Reflecting the Biblical Model,* or to purchase the book entitled *Problem Solvers and Soul Winners: A Handbook for Deacons and Deaconesses,* use the following contact information to place an order:

AVA's Book Publishers
109 Ellacott Drive
Huntsville, Alabama 35806
(256) 722-8988 or (256) 656-6099
www.avasbookpublishers.com